T0197147

To my grandchildren:
Hannah, Noah, Eliza and Samuel

Contents

Introduction ix

Chapter 1: Hearth and Home 1
Chevy Chase (April 1946 – September 1956)

Chapter 2: The City of Lights...................................... 9
Paris (October 1951 – April 1952)

Chapter 3: The Heart of Darkness.............................. 14
Léopoldville (October 1956 – December 1958)

Chapter 4: The Gold Coast.. 28
Accra (September 1960 – September 1961, plus Summer 1962)

Chapter 5: The Eternal City 35
Rome (September 1961 – June 1963)

Chapter 6: As Time Goes By 43
Casablanca (Vacations 1963 – 1967)

Chapter 7: Homeward Bound 52
Temporarily (1963 – 1972)

Chapter 8: Pearl of the Orient..75
Manila (August 1972 – March 1986)

Chapter 9: Back to the Future 98
Geneva (April 1986 – July 1995)

Chapter 10: The Long Road Home...114
Forever (July 1995 – Present)

Epilogue 168

Introduction

Dear Reader,

Growing up, I knew only one of my grandparents: my widowed maternal grandmother, Elsie Mendell Hall. As you will discover in my early chapters, Grandmother Elsie played an important role in my young life. As a child, I learned bits and pieces about her from overheard conversations. Two of the things that stayed with me were that she was a college graduate and a Latin teacher. Most of my elementary school friends' mothers and grandmothers were stay-at-home moms. While I understood my grandmother was unusual, it never occurred to me to ask her about the details of her life.

I wish I had known Grandmother Elsie when I was older and while her memories were still intact. (She suffered from dementia and spent the last 18 years of her life in nursing homes.) Born in 1880, she had witnessed firsthand so many momentous historical events: the women's suffrage movement, two world wars, the 1918 Spanish flu pandemic, and the Great Depression, just to name a few. I would have liked to have asked her how these events had affected her personally. Her life spanned nearly a century — she died one week short of her 97th birthday — and I regret not having heard her tell her personal stories.

I wanted a different legacy for my own grandchildren. Over the years, we've spent time together in their hometowns (Portland, Oregon, and Houston, Texas) and in San Diego, where they visited me nearly every summer from the time they could fly as unaccompanied minors until the pandemic hit. My grandchildren will undoubtedly have good memories of the times we shared, especially Hannah, who traveled with me to France, Switzerland, and Iceland when she was 12. While we've never been at a loss for conversation, like me with my grandmother, they've never heard many of the stories of my past.

I decided I should document my stories for them, and for all my friends, who constantly tell me, "You should write a book!" whenever they hear a snippet about some faraway place. Unsure of where to begin, on January 25, 2020, I started attending weekly memoir writing classes through San Diego Writers, Ink. (This was the same week that the CDC confirmed the first coronavirus case in the U.S. but before widespread acknowledgment of a global pandemic.) I learned in our initial class that I was not actually writing a memoir (typically covering just a portion of a person's life) but an autobiography, from my birth to the present. This turned out unwittingly to be my pandemic project.

And what a project it was! As you will see, I've recounted my life in chapters — one for each place I lived — starting in Chevy Chase, Maryland, and ending in San Diego, California. While the bookend chapters are set in the United States, most of the locations are global. Four of them involved assignments with my family of origin (my parents and the earlier ones with my two sisters): Paris, Léopoldville, Accra, and Casablanca. Two were on my own: Rome and my first stint in Geneva. The last two, and the longest sojourns spanning nearly a quarter century, were in Manila and back in Geneva with my family by marriage (my husband and three children). Each relocation — to disparate countries at different stages of my life — presented new sets of challenges.

Some of you, dear Readers, make an appearance in this autobiography. You may feel slighted that you were not given a larger role or, worse, believe you were wrongly portrayed. Please remember that this is the story of *me*. It's told from my perspective — what I remember and what I felt. While I have written my story primarily for my grandchildren, I hope others will appreciate it as well. I trust, in reading it, you will see how I was transformed on my life's journey. Perhaps you will come to understand how I felt — and continue to feel — at home almost anywhere but with nowhere to truly call home.

Happy reading, Sybilla

San Diego, California
July 1, 2021

Hearth and Home

Chevy Chase (April 1946 – September 1956)

Home. It's a small word — only four letters, but perfectly balanced with two consonants and two vowels. Its aspirated sound is often not much louder than a whisper. But it speaks volumes. So much meaning is embedded in this one word. It can connote a geographic location, like a country or a town, or a specific dwelling place. It has spawned innumerable popular sayings, like "Home is where the heart is," and "There is no place like home." For me, 3803 Bradley Lane, Chevy Chase, Maryland, was home — both a hometown and a residence — for the first 10 years of my life. At the time, the child that I was didn't understand the significance of this. I just knew it was where I lived with my parents and two older sisters from the day I was brought home from the hospital.

It wasn't until I started living overseas that the concept of home began to crystalize. The farther I traveled and the longer I stayed away, the more important Chevy Chase became as a symbol of something greater than a two-story house on Bradley Lane. And it was during these extended absences that I learned in heartbreaking ways what it meant to be "homesick."

It was a longing for a place and a house, yes, but above all, a longing for the naïve little girl who had not yet been torn from her moorings and who had not yet had to adjust and adapt to what seemed to be countless new places.

3803 Bradley Lane, Chevy Chase, Maryland

The house at #3803 was white-shingled with green shutters and a Southern-style front porch that wrapped around one of its sides. It was built in 1912. The graveled driveway that exited off Bradley Lane split in two, one section going straight back toward the detached garage and the other curving slightly up to the front steps of the house. Along the driveway to the house was a low hedge of boxwood, evergreen shrubs often planted in elegant and formal gardens in Europe but that seemed perfectly suited to our front yard. The hedge was the right height for jumping over, even though at certain times of the year, its aroma was unappealingly pungent. There were five steps leading up to the front door. One of my favorite photographs is of Grandmother Elsie and me at about five years old sitting on the second step; she is reading a book to me, and for once in a photo, I am not frowning.

With Grandmother Elsie, circa 1951

The front door opened into a foyer with a staircase that went up to the second floor. It was sparsely furnished, with just an upright piano to one side, a rug, and a small table by the side of the front door with a silver tray for the calling cards of visitors. This Victorian tradition had died decades earlier, but the tray remained as a symbol of what it meant to live an upper-class life. The living room was to the left off the foyer and the dining room to the right; both rooms had front-facing windows, with the kitchen and pantry hidden away behind the dining room.

Upstairs were five bedrooms: one for my parents, one for each of my sisters and me, and a guest room that was occupied several months of the year by Grandmother Elsie. I don't remember anyone else ever staying there. The six of us shared one bathroom on the second floor, supplemented by a small powder room downstairs. An unfinished attic was used for storage, and an unfinished basement for laundry, which was done with an old-fashioned wringer washing machine. There was no dryer; clotheslines ran the length of the basement, and a small room off to the side had an ironing board and iron. Five days a week, our maid, Susie Townsend, did the housework, laundry, and cooking, as well as took on the role of nanny: giving us snacks when we came home from school and making sure we did our homework.

I loved my bedroom. The walls were painted pale yellow, and it had windows on two sides, one overlooking the backyard, which had a square trellis and garden beds of roses, and the other facing a neighbor's house at relatively close quarters considering the lot sizes in Chevy Chase. My room was small and sparsely furnished, just a single bed, bedside stand, and chest of drawers. I don't remember any decorations: no curtains, no artwork on the walls, and no knickknacks cluttering the surfaces. But it was mine, all mine. It was the place I could go and shut the door and stay in my own little world. I could escape the bullying of my two older sisters and the raised voice of my mother as she picked on my father for some real or imagined transgression. He secretly called her "Old Faithful," referring to the geyser located in Yellowstone National Park, known for its frequent eruptions.

Our house was walking distance to the border of the District of Columbia and a five-mile drive to the White House along Connecticut Avenue. Chevy Chase is one of the wealthiest communities in the U.S. It's surprising that this is where we lived because my family was not wealthy, far from it. My father — James Frederick Green — was a civil servant and received a modest government salary. My mother didn't start working until my sisters and I were all in school. My parents had to stretch financially to purchase our house in Chevy Chase — their first house — for $15,000 in early 1945 (it's now worth close to $3 million). They were house poor, and I grew up feeling deprived in our affluent community. Our neighbors across the street, the Pages, were members of the exclusive Chevy Chase Club, a stone's throw away, and among the first to fly across country to visit Disneyland when it opened in the summer of 1955. In contrast, we didn't even own a television set to watch the Mickey Mouse Club.

The first 10 years of my life, all but six months spent in Chevy Chase, were not particularly happy ones. I got off to a rocky start, being abandoned when I was only hours old.

My mother — Henrietta Hall Green — gave birth to me at Suburban Hospital in Bethesda, Maryland, at 3:10 in the morning of Good Friday, one of the most somber days of the year for a faithful Christian like her. But her black mood had nothing to do with the remembrance of Jesus's crucifixion; it had to do with me, her third daughter who was supposed to be her first son. Besides being the wrong gender, I was premature, underweight, scrawny, bald, and scowling, not looking even remotely like the plump and smiling Gerber baby she must have conjured up while she was pregnant with me. She allegedly took one look at me and refused to have anything to do with me. She would not hold me or breastfeed me or even let me stay in her room. I was relegated to the hospital nursery, where the nurses convinced some of the breastfeeding mothers there to serve as wet nurses to me until they could bring my mother around. Today, my mother would have undoubtedly been diagnosed with severe postpartum depression, but back then, she must have been stigmatized as a bad mother.

With my mother, Henrietta Hall Green, circa 1946

I would like to think that things got better once I was brought home from the hospital, but I somehow doubt it. As the third child, there are not many photographs of me. On the back of one with my mother holding me at a few months old, she scribbled in pencil a comment about how fat she looked — nothing about how cute I was in my little sun suit. She struggled with her weight her entire adult life, and the postpartum hormones had undoubtedly made things worse for her. She was unhappy with me, unhappy with herself, perpetually unhappy with my father, and unhappy with life itself. How she kept her sanity during my early elementary school years was by escaping hearth and home to immerse herself in intellectually stimulating work as a research librarian at The Johns Hopkins University's Operations Research Office (later Research Analysis Corporation).

While my mother's parenting skills left a lot to be desired, I was nurtured by three amazing women — Grandmother Elsie, our maid, Susie Townsend, and our neighbor Mary Page. All three took time to cater to my needs: reading and playing card games with my grandmother, caring and feeding from Susie, and open-armed mothering from Mrs. Page, who had three daughters of her own but warmly welcomed one more into her fold. For my sixth birthday, she sewed me a beautiful pinafore, hand-embroidered with "Now We Are Six" and characters from the *Winnie-the-Pooh* book. She also sewed for me my very first dress that didn't come from the secondhand store or a hand-me-down from my sisters.

I spent an outrageous amount of time at the Pages' house, but no one seemed to mind. Even when I was home, I was virtually invisible and, as the youngest, often excluded from my older sisters' activities. Once, the two of them got to go with the older Page girls to a taping of *The Howdy Doody Show* for television while I had to stay home. (Each show began with the show's host, Buffalo Bob, asking the peanut gallery of about 40 children, "Say kids, what time is it?" The kids yelled back in unison, "It's Howdy Doody Time!" and then sang the show's theme song.) How I wanted to be one of those kids. I locked myself in our downstairs powder room and cried for hours.

With Susie Townsend, Gloucester, summer 1947

And where was my father during the first 10 years of my life? He was living in his own world of words (and puns) and intellectual ideals. He was excruciatingly shy and introverted, much preferring to read or write than to socialize. He received both his B.A. and Ph.D. from Yale University (1932 and 1937, respectively). As a senior at Yale, he was Chairman of the Intercollegiate Disarmament Council and sent to Geneva, where he addressed a plenary session of the Conference on the Limitation and Reduction of Armaments. While completing his Ph.D., he taught at Mount Holyoke College, where my mother worked as a librarian. In retrospect, my father probably should have stayed in academia; his personality was much better suited to being a college professor than a diplomat. But his passion for human rights propelled him into public service. He witnessed the signing of the charter that established the United Nations in 1945, attended all but one session of the U.N. General Assembly from 1946 to 1955, and served as an advisor to Eleanor Roosevelt. I was 10 when he joined the Foreign Service, and our diplomatic life began. Before that, my father had been busy with his work at the

State Department during the week, listening to opera on the radio on Saturday afternoons and gardening in our backyard, tending to his award-winning roses.

Green family, Chevy Chase, Christmas 1946

On the surface, we looked like a typical American family, perhaps even a Norman Rockwell one as we sat together in a pew near the front of All Saints' Episcopal Church on Sunday mornings or ate meat-and-potato meals seated around our large, round dining room table. Our family was White, Anglo-Saxon (my father's ancestors were Irish, my mother's British), and Protestant, as WASP-y as you get, with a strong emphasis on education and the pedagogy of John Dewey. WASPs were known to be "emotionally constipated," and my parents fit that bill. My father was emotionally absent, and my mother was capable of expressing only one emotion: anger. They were not demonstrative or affectionate, either to each other or to us children. I longed to be hugged and kissed and cuddled but never was. We were a family in form but not in substance. What little connection we had slowly eroded over the years and eventually disintegrated almost entirely in the late 1950s in the "Heart of Darkness" along the banks of the Congo River.

CHAPTER 2

The City of Lights

Paris (October 1951 – April 1952)

When I was five years old, my favorite book was *Madeline* by Ludwig Bemelmans. The storybook Madeline wasn't much like me: she was older by two years, a redhead, and French, but for some reason, she appealed to me. I was fascinated that she lived in a boarding school "in an old house in Paris that was covered in vines." It seemed all the more real to me because my older sister Kathy had recently had her appendix out, and I, like the 11 other girls in the story, wanted mine out, too. I knew nothing about the surgery, but it certainly seemed to garner a lot of attention for the patient! I didn't know how to read *Madeline* by myself, but I spent hours looking at the pictures and waiting for Grandmother Elsie to read to me. She was infinitely patient with me and never seemed to mind reading the same book over and over again.

It was understandable then that I would be ecstatic when, in the summer of 1951, I heard we would be going to Paris to live for six months. My father would be part of Eleanor Roosevelt's delegation to the 6th session of the U.N. General Assembly to be held in Paris from November 1951 to February 1952. Afterward, he would stay in Geneva during the week while Eleanor Roosevelt was attending meetings of the Human Rights Commission and return to Paris by train on weekends. My father usually traveled on his own all over the world, including to Canberra, Australia, in 1947 for the South Seas Conference. But this time my mother is reported to have put her foot down and said, "We are all going or nobody is going." She was very strong-willed; few argued with her and won.

A few months later, in early October, my father left for France with the U.S. delegation, sailing on the *America* in first class. My mother followed on the *Queen Mary*, in third class, with her mother and my sisters and me. She had worked at a local department store selling hats and rented our house in Chevy Chase in order to finance our trip. I remember so many things about our Atlantic crossing: the playroom, elaborate meals in the dining room, children's movies in the theater, emergency drills standing on deck in our life jackets, and more. (In 2017, I visited the *Queen Mary*, now permanently docked in Long Beach. While many parts of the ship had been remodeled, I found most everything, including the playroom, as I remember it.)

With my sisters, on the deck of the Queen Mary, *October 1951*

Once in Paris, my mother found a beautiful furnished apartment on the rue Jean Goujon in the heart of the "Golden Triangle" in Paris's 8th arrondissement, not far from the Champs-Elysées. It was so spacious and well-appointed that Eleanor Roosevelt would take it over for her private soirées. Such an apartment would be exorbitantly expensive today, but this was only six years after the end of World War II, and France was still recovering economically. The slow economy also explains why we were able to attend a private French school, have a cook/cleaner work for us, and eat leisurely Sunday lunches at fashionable Parisian restaurants.

I loved Paris (and still do). I have fond memories of seeing the landmarks, like the Eiffel Tower, which was featured on the cover of the *Madeline* book. As I was in kindergarten, I only went to school in the mornings; in the afternoons, my grandmother walked me around the streets, the markets, and the parks of Paris. My favorite was the Tuileries Garden, located between the Louvre and the Place de la Concorde. Sometimes on weekends, the whole family would go to the Tuileries Garden. It had an old-fashioned carousel. As we rode around, we tried to grab hold of a brass ring with our wooden stick. My sisters, being taller than me, were usually more successful in catching the brass ring. I was always extremely frustrated after our rides. We also sailed our model sailboats in the Tuileries Garden fountain. Once in mid-winter, my sister Kathy fell into the fountain and had to be rushed home before she got hypothermia. Once again, as when Kathy had her appendix out, I was jealous of all the attention she got. I don't recall ever being the center of my family's attention. (When I took my then 12-year-old granddaughter, Hannah, to Paris in 2015, I insisted we visit the Tuileries Garden after our tour of the Louvre. I was delighted to see little had changed in the intervening decades.)

Riding the carousel at the Tuileries Garden, winter 1951

What I didn't love about Paris was my school. It was run by French nuns, not at all as empathetic as Madeline's Miss Clavel. In fact, some of them were downright cruel. No one spoke English, and I had yet to learn French. My sister Eleanor had tried to teach me a few words of vocabulary on the ship, but she was already on the letter P in her flashcards, so I learned words like "papillon" (butterfly), "pamplemousse" (grapefruit), "parapluie" (umbrella), and "pantoufles" (slippers). I liked the sound of these words, but they weren't at all helpful when I needed to ask my teacher if I could go to the restroom. I got increasingly frustrated at not being able to communicate and having my hand swatted with a ruler when I colored outside the lines. I began to act out and cry at the top of my lungs; the nuns would have to call one of my sisters to the classroom to calm me down. On one occasion, I actually kicked one of the nuns: she wanted me to take off my boots, but it was cold in the classroom, and she was still wearing hers. I'm sure the nuns sighed in relief when our six months' stay was up and we left their school.

Despite my negative school experience, I was devastated when we had to leave Paris and return to the States, this time crossing the Atlantic on the *Queen Elizabeth*. The City of Lights was at its most beautiful: spring had arrived, and all the flowers were in full bloom.

The Tuileries Garden looked magical with plot after plot of colorful tulips and the striking *Cercis* trees with their heart-shaped leaves and pinkish-red blossoms. I would miss the walks with my grandmother with stops at the *boulangerie* (bakery) for baguettes, which I would nibble on as we walked home, or the *pâtisserie* (pastry shop), where we would linger over cups of hot chocolate and occasionally a croissant or other delectable snack.

Even though I was only five, I remember minute details about that six-month stay in Paris better than the subsequent years back in Chevy Chase. Living in that amazing European capital made an indelible impression on my young mind and triggered a lifelong desire to travel to other countries. Little did I know, however, that the next foreign country I would call home would be a developing African country, nothing at all like France. Indeed, we were to head to the heart of colonial Africa, where poverty, disease, and injustice were rampant, and political upheaval was simmering just below the surface.

Postscript: When we came back from Paris, I was enrolled in Rosemary Elementary School, initially for the last couple of months of kindergarten and then continuously until I finished third grade and we left for my father's first African assignment.

Third grade class photo (fall 1955). I am at the center of the first row.

CHAPTER

3

The Heart of Darkness

Léopoldville (October 1956 – December 1958)

When I was little, our family had a globe. It was a beautiful globe, perched on its axis, with interesting cartographic features, including azure-colored oceans and rivers and raised relief to show mountain ranges. On it were indicated at least a thousand place names. I spent hours poring over that globe, fantasizing about all the places I would visit. (Be careful what you wish for!) I knew from the globe that Australia was on the opposite side of the earth from Chevy Chase, where I lived, although when we kids dug in the backyard, we always said we would reach China.

I was familiar with the geography and topography of Africa. Its exotic-sounding place names like Ouagadougou and Timbuktu fascinated me. I had heard about the African explorers, like David Livingstone and Henry Morton Stanley. I knew the largest desert in the world was the Sahara Desert in northern Africa. I also knew the Congo rainforest was the second largest in the world after the Amazon. In short, I knew more about Africa than the average American 10-year-old. Nonetheless, I was flummoxed when my father announced at dinner one night that we would be moving to Léopoldville for at least two years.

On my 10ᵗʰ birthday, with Foxie, April 1956

I quickly learned that Léopoldville (now Kinshasa) was the capital of the Belgian Congo, an enormous country, literally at the heart of Africa. It had been a Belgian colony since 1908 and would remain one until independence in 1960, six months after we left. This was to be the first of my father's three overseas assignments since joining the Foreign Service. His position was Consul General at the U.S. Consulate in Léopoldville, also responsible for Belgian-controlled Ruanda-Urundi (now two separate countries, Rwanda and Burundi) and the Portuguese colony Angola.

My father's stunning announcement came in the summer of 1956. I had just completed third grade. With the exception of six months of kindergarten in Paris, I had never lived overseas. Chevy Chase had always been my home, and I had made some close friends, both at school and in my neighborhood. I didn't want to leave, and I especially didn't want to separate from our maid, Susie, who had practically raised me. After all, Susie was the one who waited for me when I came home from school, served me hot sweetened tea and cinnamon toast, listened to the accounts of my day, and comforted me when I needed it. I kept asking if we really had to go. In the end, my desire to travel, which remains with me even now, won over. I began to get excited about the adventure ahead of us, especially once I knew Grandmother Elsie and our dog Foxie, both of whom I adored, would be going with us.

My father was convinced that we couldn't be good ambassadors for the United States unless we had seen its "spacious skies," "amber waves of grain," and so on. The five of us — my father, mother, two sisters, and I — piled into our station wagon and headed west, with nothing but a printed atlas of road maps to guide us. We drove almost all the way across the country, turning around only after we reached the Grand Canyon. The trip was awe-inspiring for all of us: we witnessed the vastness of the western plains and the splendor of the Grand Tetons. We visited touristy landmarks, like the Steamboat Geyser in Yellowstone National Park. But we also stayed in small towns and met people who were invariably outgoing, friendly, and helpful. We spent the remaining weeks before our departure at our summer cottage in Gloucester, Massachusetts, shopping at its only large department store, Brown's, for two years' worth of clothes, shoes, and toiletries.

The cottage in Gloucester, Massachusetts

The distance from Chevy Chase to Léopoldville is 6,531 miles. In the 1950s, a plane — often a DC-6 with piston engines — could not fly that distance directly. It had to refuel frequently along the way. Moreover, my father needed to stop in Brussels and Lisbon to get credentialed from the governments of Belgium and Portugal. We flew out of New York Idlewild Airport (now JFK) with stops in Gander and the Azores before reaching Europe. I was so excited: this was my first time to fly. I was literally jumping up and down in my seat for the first hour of our flight. In those days, the planes had nine single sleeping berths that could be lowered from overhead. Our family had five of those nine berths, so we flew in relative comfort across the Atlantic. I even slept in my pajamas! However, without any inflight entertainment or other distractions, except food, the trip seemed excruciatingly long. We then traveled down the west coast of Africa, again with frequent stops, with one last stop to the east in Kano, Nigeria, before safely reaching Léopoldville. (We were lucky: that same month, Pan Am Flight 6 went down in the Pacific Ocean after two of its four engines failed.)

A staff member from the U.S. Consulate met us at the airport in Léopoldville, shepherded us through customs, and ushered us into our car, a black sedan with consular license plates and two small American flags flying on either side of the hood. It was the first time I experienced what it meant to be a diplomat's daughter, and as we sped toward our official residence located on the banks of the Congo River, I was exhilarated. Our servants (as they were called then) lined up in front of our new home — a long row of men and women who would serve as our cook, butler, housemaid, laundry woman, gardener, and more. My sisters and I were running around the upstairs of the mansion, loudly squabbling over which room would be whose, when our father stopped us dead in our tracks: "This is not your house. It belongs to the U.S. Government. Keep your voices down and show some respect." This was my second experience of what it meant to be a diplomat's daughter and, sadly for us, a big damper on our childhood exuberance.

When we arrived in Léopoldville, my sister Eleanor was turning 15, my sister Kathy was 13, and I was 10. The three of us were enrolled in the Athénée Royale de Léopoldville, a Belgian school with six primary years and six secondary years. Now, several English-speaking schools, including the American School of Kinshasa and the British International School, operate in Kinshasa, but in the 1950s, few educational options existed. As the semester had already started, I was already behind and spoke only a little French and no Flemish, the second language in our bilingual curriculum. I also had never studied Latin, and my fellow classmates had started years earlier. Although the Congo is 77 times bigger than Belgium, we studied only Belgian history and geography. I was totally befuddled and stayed mute for the first six months I sat in the classroom. On the first day, I felt everyone — the teacher and other 35 students — critically watching me. After that, they left me alone. I became invisible. Fortunately, I was considered "élève non-classé" (unranked student), so my rank wasn't published in the local newspaper at the end of the term. As a former top student, I would have been mortified to have been listed #36 out of 36.

Green family, with Foxie, Léopoldville, Christmas 1956

Everything seemed strange to me, not only the languages and the curriculum but also the social order. My classmates were a mix of Belgians and Congolese, but I was not allowed to invite the latter to our house. At that time in this Belgian colony, there was an implicit apartheid. Although no specific laws imposed racial segregation, Black Congolese (with the exception of servants) were barred from the homes of Whites. As a 10-year-old, this was incomprehensible to me. I was racially colorblind and had a strong sense of social justice. As far as I was concerned, we were living in their country, and the Belgians had no right to tell them where they could go and what they could do. But, of course, as colonialists, they did as they pleased. I was even more horrified when I saw the parents of my White friends beating their servants — something I've only since witnessed in movies. My Belgian classmates seemed destined to follow in their parents' footsteps. They bullied our Congolese classmates and called them "macaques" (monkeys) behind their backs and sometimes even to their faces.

Whatever family cohesion we had when we arrived began to slowly unravel. My parents became totally enmeshed in the diplomatic life of the Congo's capital city, already a growing metropolis (now a megacity with an estimated population of nearly 12 million). They went out almost every night to cocktail parties, receptions, and dinners. My teenage sisters were both dating: Eleanor's boyfriend was a tall, blond Dutchman, and Kathy's was a dashing Australian (Léopoldville was certainly international). This was just after the release of "Rock Around the Clock" — the song in 1955 and the movie in 1956 — so the local nightclubs were in full swing every night of the week. As I watched everyone get ready to go out, I felt like Cinderella but without even a dream of a different outcome. Except for the very short time Grandmother Elsie stayed with us, I felt totally abandoned, sitting at home alone and eating dinner by myself at our enormous dining room table. I'm sure even the servants felt sorry for me. (Grandmother Elsie had initially planned to stay with us throughout our Léopoldville assignment, but was unable to tolerate the tropical heat and humidity and returned to the States prematurely.)

My utter abandonment came when I was 11: I broke my leg and was left alone in a hospital while my entire family traveled across the Congo to Ruanda-Urundi. It was a Saturday, and we had been picnicking with a group of families outside of Léopoldville. I was roller skating with some of my friends on a concrete patio when I fell and broke my right leg in two places. Of course, at the time, I didn't know it was broken. I just kept saying, "It hurts! It hurts!" My parents initially tried to trivialize my injury, insisting I wasn't crying enough for it to be serious. Had they forgotten they had brought us all up to be stoics? Eventually, they decided to take me to an emergency room back in the city. No doctor was on duty, so they took me home for the night, and we returned the next day. They rushed off to go to church and left me there without signing a consent form for anesthesia, so I experienced excruciating pain while the doctor set my twice-broken tibia and applied a cast from the top of my thigh down to my toes.

Once my leg was set and I was settled in my hospital room, the family took off on their trip, driving our station wagon more than 1,000 miles on unpaved, potholed roads and visiting American missionary families along the way. I was left with hospital staff, who spoke no French, only Lingala and Kikongo, two of the four Indigenous languages that have the status of a national language in the Congo. As my leg was in traction and I couldn't get out of bed, I have never felt more helpless or bereft in my life. The ache of aloneness hurt almost as much as my leg did. I quickly learned a few words of each language to ask for water or food or a bedpan. Every few days someone from the U.S. Consulate would visit me. However, during the weeks I was on my own, my family was out in the boondocks and unable to even call to see how I was doing.

After my discharge from the hospital, I flew with a family friend to Stanleyville (now Kisangani) to meet my parents and sisters on their way back from their trip. The man who accompanied me was an artist and painted a gorgeous giraffe the length of the back of my cast, which looked great only when I wore shorts. I was thrilled to be reunited with my family, but we didn't stay long in Stanleyville. Almost immediately, we sailed together on a small paddle wheel boat another 1,000 miles down the Congo River back to Léopoldville.

I heard amazing stories from my parents and sisters of their road trip across the Congo and their stay in Ruanda-Urundi. Along the way, they visited villages inhabited by disparate populations, from the tall Maasai tribespeople dressed in bright red robes and armed with hunting spears to the scantily clad, short-statured Pygmies, who were more foragers than hunters. My family got to picnic on the banks of Lake Tanganyika, the longest freshwater lake in the world (410 miles) and view the incomparable topography of Central Africa — from desert-like plains to rainforests. Later, my father would travel to Luanda, the capital of Angola, to pay his respects to the other country under his Consulate. However, the highlight of all his travels, in Africa and elsewhere, was to Albert Schweitzer's hospital at Lambaréné in French Equatorial Africa (now Gabon). My father was a great admirer of Dr. Schweitzer — a theologian, organist, writer, humanitarian, philosopher, physician, and the 1952 Nobel Peace Prize winner — and was mesmerized when listening to him play Bach fugues on his organ in the middle of the jungle.

My father, representing the U.S., in a dangerous locale!

My abandonment in the hospital taught me I was a fighter and a survivor. I refused to give in to my loneliness and began to spend more and more time at the homes of friends, many of them missionaries. I was exposed to evangelical Protestantism in their homes and in Sunday school, where I had to memorize the order of the books of the Bible and lengthy passages from the New Testament. I even went on a vacation with one missionary family, driving from Brazzaville (across the river from Léopoldville) to Pointe-Noire on the Atlantic coast of French Congo. The distance is 348 miles; on today's roads, you can drive it in a little more than eight hours. Back then, on potholed dirt roads, it took four days each way.

I also pulled out all the stops to excel in home arts and physical education (both of which were graded) as well as in my academic courses. I learned how to crochet and knit. I worked out until I could climb the ropes to the top of our very tall school gym and swim faster than anyone in my age group. I tapped into every possible resource, including getting my sister's Dutch boyfriend to help me with my Flemish homework. (Dutch is the official language of the Netherlands, whereas Flemish is a dialect spoken in parts of Belgium and France.) Once I was ranked, my class standing steadily improved. Much to my Belgian classmates' chagrin, I ended up at the top of my class. Their parents didn't take kindly to the fact that an American could do better than their own children; I heard rumors that some of them had been beaten. I was no longer invisible but wished I still were. The only black mark I ever got was in "soin" (carefulness) when my father forgot to sign and return my report card. From then on, I signed them myself. I had, in effect, taken parenting into my own hands.

I had no choice. My parents paid absolutely no attention to me. I rode my bike by myself back and forth to school twice a day. In Belgian colonial style, we had a two-hour lunch break to eat and take a siesta, so two of those trips were in the scorching midday sun. Looking back, I presume kidnapping of diplomats' kids wasn't a problem, but it seems it might have been risky. My friends and I played regularly in the large rainwater sewers that flowed into the Congo River at the edge of our yard. Several times, we were almost harmed, including once by DDT sprayed into the sewer and once by a flash flood after an unexpected rainstorm. Other dangers included crocodiles wandering into our yard, mamba snakes hanging down from our trees, and diseases like schistosomiasis and onchocerciasis (river blindness) from swimming in the river.

With the benefit of time — some 60 years in this case — my sojourn in the Congo seems a bit surreal. It could be the work of fiction, like Barbara Kingsolver's *The Poisonwood Bible*. (The author's family lived in the Congo in 1963 when she was 7; her father was a physician working in a remote village.) In fact, Barbara Kingsolver's fiction parallels our nonfiction life in many ways. There were four daughters in *The Poisonwood Bible* — Rachel, 15; twins Leah and Adah, 14; and Ruth May, 5. (We were 15, 13, and 10.) They, too, lived in the Congo on the brink of civil war, and they, too, had a rather oblivious father. Mirroring the conflict in the Congo, their family, like ours, begins to disintegrate. Fortunately, I, as the youngest, was not killed by a green mamba snake like Ruth May but easily could have been.

I consider myself lucky: I left the Congo two years and two months older and considerably wiser. I returned home with many gifts: several new languages (French, Flemish, Latin, and a smattering of local Congolese dialects), knowledge of two countries (Belgium and the Congo), familiarity with the Bible from my missionary friends, and pride in myself for having made it to the top of my class. I was still introverted, shy, and fearful, but a lot less so. I was sad to be returning home without our dog, Foxie; he succumbed to a crocodile attack and was buried under a flame tree on the edge of the Congo River.

Postscript

When we returned home from the Congo, I was turning 13 and placed in Leland Junior High School, while my sisters went to Bethesda-Chevy Chase High School. Note to relocating parents: Never transfer your kids in the middle of the school year, especially if they are teenagers and it's an international move. It's a recipe for disaster. I was totally out of it — I still wore my hair in pigtails for goodness' sake — and was teased mercilessly with taunts like "Congo Bongo" and questions about cannibals. My classmates were clueless about Africa, and I was clueless about being an American teenager. I was rescued by a fellow international traveler, Ann Miller, and her mother, Janet, who had better sense than my mother did about the way I should look to my sophisticated classmates. Janet took me to the hairdresser with her daughter to have my hair cut in a stylish bob. I stopped by the Millers' house every morning on my walk to school and changed into clothes I borrowed from Ann. Her box-pleated skirts were definitely shorter than mine and the bodices of her sweaters more form-fitting. She even lent me nylon stockings and mascara. Because I stopped by her house on my way home to change back to my own things, my parents were never the wiser.

What I remember most about this time back in the States is my father's obsessive consumption of musical culture. When we went to the Congo, he shipped a piano, a phonograph, and boxes full of vinyl records, which were all housed in a small study, the only airconditioned room in our Léopoldville house. When my father wasn't working or attending diplomatic functions, he could be found sitting in the study listening to music — operas, Gilbert and Sullivan operettas, Broadway musicals, popular tunes, and comedic pieces sung by the satirist Tom Lehrer. My father said repeatedly that when he retired, he was going to move to New York City and go to a musical performance almost every night of the week. (He eventually did just that but only after my mother died in 1973.)

On this home leave, we attended an incredible number of operas and concerts. In the summer, the concerts were held outdoors at the Carter Barron Amphitheatre, located in Rock Creek Park. There, I had the honor of hearing in person some of the musical greats of all time — the Kingston Trio, Henry Mancini, Nat King Cole, Harry Belafonte, Louis Armstrong, and Ella Fitzgerald. When a local movie theater featured a week-long festival of Broadway musicals, my father took time off from work, and he and I went to two movies every day, one in the morning and one in the afternoon. We saw more than a dozen musicals in a row, including some from the early 1950s, like *An American in Paris* and *Annie Get Your Gun*, and others released the summer we left for the Congo, like *High Society* and *The King and I.* This was a special time for me; I was able to bond with my father on my own. I felt like a VIP. My father went on to give an immensely popular lecture entitled "The History of the Anglo-American Musical" to audiences in Africa through the U.S. Information Agency's cultural program.

This time back in the U.S. was a homecoming of sorts. We were technically home, but our house on Bradley Lane was still rented out. We ended up camping out in a semi-furnished apartment near Bethesda-Chevy Chase High School. We eventually moved back in to #3803 but only briefly. Our entire stay in the U.S. lasted less than 20 months. I completed eighth grade at Leland before we were transferred to our second African posting in Accra, Ghana. I never again went back to live at our house on Bradley Lane, in what had been my home for the first 10 years of my life. From then on, I visited only occasionally and briefly, such as when I got married and the reception was held in the yard. I had been torn from my moorings early on and, from the time I was a teen, was officially without a permanent home and rootless.

CHAPTER

4

The Gold Coast

Accra (September 1960 – September 1961,
plus Summer 1962)

When my parents and I arrived in Ghana in September 1960, I was 14 years old and, for the first time in my life, an only child. My two older sisters had set out on their own. Eleanor had started Vassar College (following in the footsteps of Grandmother Elsie, class of 1901, and our mother, class of 1932). Kathy stayed behind to finish her last year and graduate from Bethesda-Chevy Chase High School. My father was the newly appointed Deputy Chief of Mission at the U.S. Embassy in the capital, Accra. (He would serve as Chargé d'Affaires in between ambassadors from November 1960 to January 1961 and from March to June 1962.) As we stepped off the plane at the Accra International Airport (later renamed Kotoka), an entourage from the embassy met us, whisked us through immigration and customs, and drove us to our official residence.

I felt like Dorothy in the *Wizard of Oz*. One day I was living an ordinary American life, attending a suburban junior high school, and the next, I was suddenly being transported to another land. Ghana was as foreign to me as Oz was to Dorothy.

Ghana had become independent from the British on March 6, 1957 — a little more than four years before our arrival — with President Kwame Nkrumah as its leader. The former Gold Coast was considered one of the most advanced of Britain's African colonies, one reason it was the first to be granted independence. Even to my 14-year-old eyes, Ghana seemed light years ahead of the Belgian Congo, the only other African country I had visited. I had mixed feelings about being plunked down in Ghana. On the one hand, I was happy to escape Leland Junior High School, where I never really fit in. On the other, I didn't feel ready to make yet another major adjustment.

Shortly after our arrival, I was placed in Ghana International School (GIS). At that time, GIS was newly established and had only about 200 students, mostly British teenagers who had not done well enough on their 13-plus common entrance exam to study in the U.K. GIS was international in name only; the curriculum was exclusively British and geared to Britain's national exams. My few classmates and I studied nothing related to Ghana, and the courses would undoubtedly not prepare me to attend college in the U.S. (The American International School in Accra wouldn't open for another half century.)

I was bored to tears at school and lonely at home. My parents were always out at diplomatic functions: I counted 40 nights in a row that they weren't home, and the first night they were, we had guests. They did a lot of entertaining at home, including showing delayed newsreels of the four presidential debates of 1960, John F. Kennedy versus Richard Nixon. Hundreds of people gathered in our large garden to watch these debates projected on a white sheet strung up on a wall. While the Ghanaians were generally more interested in local and British politics, the young and dashing JFK had created quite a buzz in Accra. (Once he was inaugurated as president, Kennedy invited President Nkrumah for a state visit to Washington in March 1961.) My parents encouraged me to attend as many of these functions as I liked even though I was only 14. There, they introduced me to drinking and smoking. In those days, the health risks of cigarettes were unknown, but still ... I would continue smoking for more than a decade, until I was pregnant with my first child.

Sometime during that academic year, what was the middle of my ninth grade, I just stopped going to school. Every morning, either my mother or my father would knock on my bedroom door, open it a crack, and announce, "It's time to go to school." And every morning, I would pull the sheet up over my head and shout, "I'm not going." Appearances were everything in the diplomatic service, and I guess they decided it wouldn't look proper to drag me into the classroom. Instead, I spent my days at the beach and my evenings out with my much older boyfriend, Ken, who was a Marine guard at the U.S. Embassy. Barbie doll's boyfriend, Ken, was just being marketed (March 1961), and the original 12-inch doll could have been modeled on my real-life Ken: tall, blond, blue-eyed, with ridiculously broad shoulders and narrow waist. Both looked great in their dress blues! Unlike my parents, I wasn't concerned that Ken hadn't gone to college and had little ambition beyond completing his Marine Corps service and returning to his hometown of Omaha, Nebraska. My parents kept telling me things like, "You deserve someone with more gumption than Ken," or "You would be bored to tears in Omaha." In retrospect, they were probably right, but at the time, I wasn't willing to concede this or anything else to them.

Ghana has more than 300 miles of coastline and some of the most beautiful sandy beaches in the world. It was the place of one of the iconic scenes in the 1966 movie *Endless Summer*, and its beaches have since become a hotspot for surfing in West Africa. When I was hanging out on the beaches near Accra, we didn't have the Hawaiian-style longboards. We surfed on short, thin plywood boards — similar to today's skim boards — and we rode the waves lying down, like a body surfer. I had perpetual bruising along my midsection from not pulling up the front of my board fast enough after cresting over a wave and ending up planted in the sand.

The bikini bathing suit was just starting to become popular, especially in France, and I was one of the first to buy one in Accra at the Kingsway Department Store. My mother, when she saw what

I was wearing under my see-through coverup, was livid. "There's no way a daughter of mine will be seen in public wearing what looks like skimpy underwear," she railed. When I refused to change into my conservative, one-piece bathing suit, she slapped me across the face. It was the first and only time I remember her doing so. The slap was painful, but not nearly as excruciating as the sunburn I got on my previously unexposed stomach. I never told my mother about the sunburn; she would have had the last laugh. I continued to wear a bikini to the beach in Accra and later when we lived in Casablanca. By then, the bikini had become more mainstream and my mother less resistant. But in the early 1960s, my bikini wearing was a symbol of my adolescent rebelliousness.

My parents were at their wits' end. They had never had to deal with a defiant school dropout before. Education was a priority for them. They began to look into options to get me back into the classroom. Boarding school outside of Ghana seemed to be the only viable one. (My sister Kathy had been homeschooled in the Belgian Congo, using correspondence courses from the Calvert School's Home Instruction Division, one of the first of its kind, with only modest success.) The potential locations were limitless — from the U.S. to Europe and from South Africa to India. We settled on Marymount International School in Rome because my friend Ann Miller was there. After our time together in Chevy Chase, her father had been posted to Kenya with USAID. Ann had been so supportive at Leland Junior High School and would continue to be at Marymount.

I was still living in Accra when, on August 30, 1961, the very first group of Americans to serve as Peace Corps volunteers (Ghana I) arrived to serve as teachers. Two days earlier, President Kennedy had hosted a send-off ceremony for them in the White House Rose Garden. My parents and I were standing on the tarmac as the charter plane carrying these volunteers landed. Not only was this a signature initiative of President Kennedy's administration, but also our cousin on my mother's side, Newell Flather, was among the 51 volunteers. Later that day, the volunteers were warmly received by President

Nkrumah — an auspicious start to their two-year sojourns in the country.

Shortly after the Peace Corps volunteers arrived, I left Ghana to attend boarding school in Rome. It wasn't until the following summer, when I returned to Ghana, that I got to know the group well. Cousin Newell was assigned to teach at the high school in the historic coastal town of Winneba, a little more than 30 miles from Accra. It wasn't an easy trip from Winneba to Accra on a local bus, about three hours, but Newell visited whenever he could for family gatherings. Coincidently, another cousin also lived in Ghana at the time: Anne Brantley Betts lived in the port city of Takoradi for four years with her family, first husband, Jim Brantley, and their four children, Beth, Bill, George, and Suzanne. Every Sunday evening, my parents had an open house for any and all Americans who were on their own or who simply wanted a home-cooked meal. Our house became a regular hangout for the Peace Corps volunteers, U.S. Embassy staff, and others. My mother epitomized what it meant to be "The Hostess with the Mostest," and she got great satisfaction in taking care of those she called "orphans" and "strays."

That summer of 1962 was a swinging one — or rather, a twisting one. The song "Let's Twist Again" had been released as a single by Chubby Checker in 1961. It was one of the biggest hit singles in the U.S. that year. Its popularity — and the Twist dance craze it spawned — slowly spread around the world, even as far away as Accra. The Peace Corps volunteers, including my cousin, who came into town on the weekends begged me to teach them this new dance. I was tickled pink to think I might have something to teach this much older and wiser cohort (they had all graduated from college). On Saturday nights, we would go to open-air nightclubs to dance both the Twist and the urban Ghanaian dance called the High Life. Both required substantial hip movements, the Twist side to side and the High Life in a forward, cha-cha-like shuffle. Fueled by enough Star Beer (the brewery had been established two years earlier), even the most uptight volunteers eventually learned to let go and dance the night away.

We were lucky. We lived in Ghana during a relatively peaceful and prosperous time. We didn't have the apartheid atmosphere that was so stifling in the Belgian Congo and were able to make Ghanaian friends. President Kwame Nkrumah was still a popular leader, although by the time we left, the unrest that led up to his overthrow in 1966 was beginning. Our family made friends that lasted a lifetime, including Anani Dzidzienyo, who later taught Africana Studies at Brown University; the Freeman family, whose son Robert (Robbie) became an artist and had works exhibited, among other places, at the Museum of Fine Arts in Boston; and above all, many of the 51 Peace Corps volunteers who made up Ghana I. My father, sister Eleanor, and I attended various reunions of Ghana I in Gloucester, hosted by Cousin Newell. The last ones I attended were the 35th and 40th anniversary reunions in the summers of 1996 and 2001, respectively, while I was still living in Boston.

I left Ghana for the last time in September 1962 to return to Rome for my final year of boarding school. My parents had not yet received their next assignment, and they were unsure of when they would be returning to the U.S. and/or be stationed elsewhere. If they returned permanently to Washington, D.C., the State Department wouldn't continue to finance my education abroad. I ended up skipping a year in order to graduate early. In retrospect, I did the right thing; otherwise, I would have started my senior year in Rome, transferred back to Washington, D.C., for a few months, and then transferred again to graduate from a French school in Casablanca, where my parents were eventually assigned. (It would not have been an American college preparatory school as none existed until three decades later.) I was getting used to being uprooted and replanted, but three different schools within one academic year would have been a bit much, especially during my senior year of high school.

When I first took off for Rome, I didn't have much to show for myself. I hadn't learned any new languages in Accra. Although more than 250 languages and dialects were spoken in Ghana, English was the official language. I didn't learn many new skills, except surfing and High Life dancing. However, I had made the transition from junior high school to high school and had matured in the process. I looked and felt much older than my 15 years. I was more than ready to leave the roost and embark on my next big adventure — this time solo.

The Eternal City

Rome (September 1961 – June 1963)

While I was well-traveled at 15, I had never flown on my own before. I was nervous when my plane touched down at Fiumicino International Airport in Rome the afternoon of Friday, September 8, 1961. The airport, sometimes referred to as "Leonardo da Vinci," had been open for less than nine months, although it had begun operations in time for the 1960 Olympics held in Rome that year. I felt totally bewildered as I entered the mammoth terminal, which was more chaotic than anything I had ever witnessed before. People were bustling around, shouting, and gesticulating at each other. I couldn't understand a word of what they said, except "scusi" whenever they jostled me as I stood frozen in place.

My mother had given me instructions on what to do when I arrived. She had lived in Rome as a teenager with her uncle and didn't think twice about sending me off on my own. I managed to make my way through the thronging crowds to collect my suitcase at baggage claim and change my American dollars into Italian lira. I headed to the taxi stand, dragging my suitcase (this was before luggage had wheels, and I didn't know how to engage the services of a porter). I clutched a piece of paper with "Via di Villa Lauchli, 180" written on it. It was the address of my new home: Marymount International School. The taxi driver deposited me unceremoniously on the front steps of the school and drove off, leaving me feeling once again alone and bewildered.

Although Rome connotes love and romance, I came to study. My plan was to graduate from high school in Italy and return to the States for college. I was entering 10th grade, even though I had never really completed 9th. Marymount, opened in 1946, was a girls' school (a mix of boarders and day students), run by the nuns of the Religious of the Sacred Heart of Mary. I was not Catholic at the time and would not have chosen it if Ann hadn't been there. Much to my relief, we ended up as roommates. I was ecstatic to be reunited with Ann, even though we were crammed into tight quarters with two other sophomores, total strangers to me. We were housed in a rose-colored, three-story building with five windows across each floor, similar in look to Madeline's storybook old house in Paris, minus the ivy.

My dormitory at Marymount International School

The flight distance from Accra to Rome is about 2,600 miles, lightyears for me. My life could not have been more different. In Accra, I came and went as I pleased. I was a beach bum by day and a party animal by night. Although I was still a young teen, my parents had long since given up parenting; once my elder sisters no longer lived at home, I was left to my own devices. Upon arriving in Rome, it was all structure and military-like discipline: rules and curfews, regulations and punishments. There were scant rewards. If we behaved during the week, we were allowed to go into Rome on Saturday mornings, and as a special perk, the senior boarders were permitted to smoke in the designated smoking room. As a non-Catholic, I was allowed to go into Rome on Sunday mornings to attend my own services at the Episcopal church, St. Paul's Within the Walls.

The transition to boarding life was tough. In the first three months, I gained 15 pounds, a combination of a more sedentary lifestyle and a high-carbohydrate diet — bread in the morning and pasta at lunch and dinner. Whatever meat we were served, usually veal, was paper-thin, and vegetables were in short supply. I quickly learned the boardinghouse reach to try to get my fair share of what was on the platter to feed an entire tableful of hungry girls. Mostly all we ate was pasta. I was not alone in my weight gain, and almost every boarder eventually developed some type of eating disorder. Yo-yo diets, anorexia, and bulimia were rampant in our dorm. I also developed a serious vitamin B deficiency and ended up having to have daily injections in my senior year.

On one of our first weekends in Rome, all of us boarders went to our affiliate boys' school, Notre Dame International, for a Living Rosary. I had never seen a rosary before, much less prayed one or witnessed a "living" one. Fifty of the girls from our school were arranged in segments of 10 (decades) around the perimeter of Notre Dame's football field, each girl representing one bead of the rosary. Between each decade were male students who led the prayers following the 10 "Hail, Mary" recitations. The 17-year-old acolyte who carried the crucifix and led the procession onto the field would become my future husband, although I had no way of knowing that at the time.

I had heard of George Dorros before I arrived in Rome, first from Ann Miller, who had met George the year before and was dating his roommate. She had mentioned him in several letters she wrote to me about life at Marymount. The Dorros family had come through Accra on their way to and from Lagos, Nigeria, where they were stationed, and people from our embassy, who learned George was studying in Rome, encouraged me to introduce myself to him once I got there.

That's exactly what I did. As the Living Rosary ended, I went up and introduced myself to George. We hit it off right away and, in the course of a short chat, realized we had a lot in common because of our fathers' careers in the Foreign Service, both specializing in African affairs. (My father was in his second out of three African postings, George's in his third out of five.) George and I agreed to meet the following Saturday morning at the American Bar, the hangout for most of the Marymount and Notre Dame students.

This was the beginning of a whirlwind three-month romance. The adage, "You've never lived until you've loved in Rome," is true! We were young, yes, but not too young to fall in love. We met every Saturday morning and some Sundays when George could get out. In between, we called each other when we could get a turn on our respective dorm phones and even wrote letters to each other (Marymount and Notre Dame were on opposite sides of the city). Whenever we got out, we spent hours walking around Rome, taking in the sights, the sounds, the smells of the city, and making memories that have literally lasted a lifetime.

When the weather permitted, we would often sit on the Spanish Steps or dangle our feet in the Trevi Fountain (before restrictions forbade such activities.) Trevi, the largest fountain in Rome, was made popular by books and movies like *Three Coins in the Fountain* (1954) and *La dolce vita* (1960). According to myth, if you throw one coin in the fountain (always with your right hand over your left shoulder), you will return to Rome. If you throw two coins, you will fall in love with an attractive Italian. If you throw three coins, you will marry that person. In my case, the myth became reality. Only the attractive Italian turned out to be an attractive Greek-American.

From left, Mike and Janet, George and me, Winter Prom, December 1961

Our whirlwind romance culminated in the Winter Prom, held the weekend before our Christmas break. It was the first time I had been to a prom, and I was thrilled by all the rituals — everything from the corsage to the ride in the limousine to the restaurant where we had dinner beforehand. The prom itself was held at Notre Dame in its beautifully decorated gym. We danced for hours to hit songs like "Run Around Sue," "Take Good Care of My Baby," and "Calendar Girl." Priests and lay chaperones stood at intervals around the gym watching that our dancing, especially to the slow songs, didn't get too intimate. Nonetheless, we were heady with the closeness of our bodies and the words of love: "Dedicated to the One I Love," and "I Love How You Love Me." There were no chaperones in the limousine when George took me back to Marymount!

The euphoria of prom night faded as dawn broke the next morning and reality slowly settled in. I had a boyfriend in Accra, and he was due to arrive in Rome in just a few days. Ken was heartbroken when I had decided to go away to boarding school. But if I had stayed in Accra, he could easily have been reassigned to an embassy in another country and I would have been the one left behind. His consolation was to come visit me in Rome during my Christmas break. We stayed in a lovely little hotel near the Borghese Gardens and celebrated Christmas at the Marine House with the Marines who were assigned to the U.S. Embassy in Rome. If anyone — my family or the nuns — found it strange that I would spend Christmas vacation alone with my boyfriend, no one let on.

I found it strange. I realized once Ken arrived that I didn't love him. We had been attracted to each other by our circumstances, expats in a foreign country with few Americans anywhere near our age and overwhelmed by loneliness. Ken had a couple of Marine buddies, but most were older than him and more worldly. Ken and I had very little in common, and that became blatantly obvious once we were alone in Rome. Nonetheless, on Christmas day, he produced a diamond engagement ring and asked me to marry him. I couldn't, just couldn't, say yes. I was still only 15 with years of education ahead of me. More importantly, my heart belonged to another.

With Ken at the Marine House, Rome, Christmas 1961

In the end, I lost both boyfriends. Ken went back to Accra even more heartbroken than when I had left in September. George found out that I had stayed in Rome over the Christmas break and was justifiably irate that I hadn't told him I had a boyfriend when I first met him. I had planned to but somehow never found the right time. In my defense, once I met George, I had decided I wasn't going to continue my relationship with Ken. However, I was reluctant to send Ken a "Dear John" letter and wanted to wait to tell him in person. I felt I owed him that. I was completely caught off guard by his marriage proposal. I tried to explain this to George when we met after Christmas break, but to no avail. Despite the many combined activities between our two high schools over the next five months, we didn't speak to each other again for more than a year.

In retrospect, it was probably just as well I didn't have a boyfriend for the rest of my time in Rome. I was able to devote myself full-time to my studies so I could skip a year in order to graduate before my parents left Ghana. I doubled up on my course load and took senior year classes, including French IV, Italian IV, and Latin IV. When I graduated in June 1963, having just turned 17, I came second in my class and earned honors in chemistry. I didn't sleep much during that time, studying by flashlight under a tent of blankets after lights out and getting up at the crack of dawn to hit the books again.

The only time I didn't study was on our mandatory tours. On Sunday afternoons, the nuns loaded all of us boarders onto buses and took us to visit the famous sights in the city and on its outskirts. Although we moaned and groaned about being shuttled around, these were wonderful opportunities to get to know Roman history and culture. During school breaks, the nuns took us farther afield. Every year we would spend Thanksgiving week in Florence, our winter break skiing in the Dolomites, and our spring break visiting different cities. I also traveled with our girls' volleyball team to places like Naples, Livorno, and Vincenza (I wasn't on the team but was allowed to go with them). The nuns would have us sightsee before and/or after the matches, such as visiting Pompeii when we were in Naples. I got to see a large swath of Italy in my two years there.

In late May 1963, when I should have been studying for final exams, the nuns took us to St. Peter's Basilica every afternoon after classes to pray for Pope John XXIII, who had stomach cancer and was dying. (He had been diagnosed in September 1962, but his diagnosis was kept from the public until near the end of his life.) We joined hundreds of others in the piazza and stood for hours reciting the Rosary, which I then knew how to pray in both English and Italian. By this time, I had decided I wanted to convert to Catholicism, but I had promised my staunchly anti-Catholic father I wouldn't while I was in Rome. I was intrigued by the rituals (priests prostrating themselves on the ground at the start of Good Friday services), the incense, the Latin mass, the statuaries in the ornate Italian churches, and the Vatican itself, with its colorful Swiss Guards and its stately pomp and ceremony.

When I finally graduated in June 1963, my parents didn't come to Rome to attend the ceremony. Instead, they had the U.S. Embassy in Rome send someone on their behalf. It was a couple I had never met before and never saw again; they seemed as uncomfortable being there as I was to have strangers celebrating my special day. I was sad to see my days at Marymount come to an end, sad to leave Rome, which I had come to love, and sad to say goodbye to my classmates and dormmates and even a couple of the nuns who had nurtured me during my two years there. I had certainly become more worldly wise and felt not a single qualm about hopping into a taxi and heading back to Fiumicino International Airport for the next leg of my journey — this time to Casablanca.

As Time Goes By

Casablanca (Vacations 1963 – 1967)

When I landed at the Mohammed V International Airport in Casablanca in the summer of 1963, I was barely 17 years old, arriving in yet another unfamiliar country. My parents were nowhere to be seen. A short, rotund man wearing a Nehru-style dark blue suit and a red fez was standing in a crowd of greeters, holding up a sign with my name on it. He waved furiously when he saw me point to his sign. He introduced himself as Haj. It was only later that I would learn that this was an honorific title since he had made the mandatory Islamic pilgrimage, or *haj*, to Mecca, Saudi Arabia. However, everyone always called him Haj; in the four years I knew him, I never learned his real name.

While I was totally ignorant about the Muslim religion, I did at least speak French, the language of France's protectorate from 1912 to 1956 and, in effect, a *lingua franca* for most Moroccans. Understanding some of the people milling around me made me feel a little less bewildered than I did on my previous solo international landing in Rome. Also, Haj had worked as a driver for the U.S. Consulate for 20 years, so he was graciously welcoming and, in retrospect, didn't seem uncomfortable being alone with an American teenager. (A Moroccan female of any age would never ride alone in a car with a man who wasn't a family member.) Haj was used to Americans and their strange ways, like parents letting a daughter travel alone. He explained that mine were busy, and he would drive me "home."

Home turned out to be the official residence of the U.S. Consul General (my father's current title). Villa Mirador was a large, gracious mansion sitting on top of a hill in a community called Anfa (the ancient toponym for Casablanca). I was duly impressed as we drove through Anfa, a leafy, upmarket residential neighborhood between the beachfront and the center of Casablanca. As we drove, Haj described our surroundings and explained that Anfa was the home of a racecourse founded in 1912 (the year the French arrived) and a nine-hole golf course. Villa Mirador was just one of many mansions in the neighborhood set in lush gardens. Haj pulled into the driveway and signaled for me to walk up the stone-paved walkway lined by palm trees to the house.

The front door of Villa Mirador was opened by a young houseboy dressed in a starched white uniform. As I stepped inside, the first thing I noticed was a beautiful octagonal dark blue-, yellow-, and white-tiled fountain, with a white marble pedestal bowl, on the left side of the carpeted staircase. I was stunned. While our official residences in Léopoldville and Accra had been grand, this was over the top; I had never had a fountain outside a house I lived in, much less inside. My curiosity was piqued, and I set off to explore my new vacation digs.

Entrance hall of the Villa Mirador, Casablanca

The first door I opened off the foyer happened to be Churchill's Map Room. British Prime Minister Winston Churchill lived in our house during the Casablanca Conference, held in January 1943 at the Hotel Anfa across the street. During the conference, U.S. President Franklin Roosevelt and Churchill met to plan the Allied European strategy for the next phase of World War II. Churchill had a "war room" filled with maps of all the theaters of war. (After the war, the United States purchased Villa Mirador from its original owner.) My father, worried that the historical significance of this so-called Map Room would be forgotten, had had a bronze plaque engraved and hung in the room. I was born after World War II, but I had studied European history and, for the first time, felt a connection to it.

I discovered which of the many bedrooms was mine since the houseboy had discreetly placed my luggage inside. Before I could begin to unpack, my parents breezed in, dressed to the nines, from some diplomatic function. They seemed almost confused to see me. I had been away at boarding school in Rome for the last two years, and they had barely seen me during that time. (We had last met briefly in December 1962, when my sister Kathy got married in Washington, D.C.) Despite our long separation, I was not treated as a returning prodigal daughter but more like one of the many houseguests who turned up at Villa Mirador that summer. For my part, they seemed like a benevolent aunt and uncle. They were planning to pay for my college education, starting in a few months, and some of my living expenses in Casablanca (I would be working and earning most of my own pocket money). We embraced in the European style: air kisses to each other's cheeks, not the hearty hugs I had conjured up on my flight coming "home." The next thing I knew, my parents were rushing to their room to change their clothes for yet another diplomatic function. The cook had instructions to bring me dinner on a tray to my room.

All in all, I spent a dozen vacations in Casablanca. I came home to visit my parents three times a year (summer, Christmas, and spring breaks) throughout my three years at Sarah Lawrence College and junior year abroad in Geneva. The vacations have all started to run together in my mind since there wasn't much to differentiate them. During most of these vacations, I worked at the General Tire & Rubber Company, headquartered in Akron, Ohio. It had started operating in Casablanca in 1961, making passenger car, truck, and tractor tires. The workers were all French-speaking Moroccans, while the managers were non-French-speaking Americans from Akron. They had only a handful of staff who spoke both languages and were delighted to have me serve as a bilingual secretary whenever I was visiting. I was respected and well paid for the work I did — drafting and translating letters and conveying instructions from a manager to a foreman. I don't remember any of the Americans trying to learn French, much less Arabic, while many of the workers were eager to learn English.

As this was a Muslim country, the factory and offices were closed on Friday. This meant that I had a day off and could accompany my parents to Rabat, the capital city, about 50 miles north of Casablanca. As Consul General, my father had to attend a weekly staff meeting at the U.S. Embassy in Rabat. My mother went along with him in order to shop at the commissary. She would fill up our official car with products she couldn't find in Casablanca or were more expensive on the local market, like toilet paper, paper towels, and maple syrup. Afterward, we would have lunch at the residence of the Deputy Chief of Mission, Leon Dorros, and his wife, Marie, who years later would become my parents-in-law. They lived in Rabat with their daughter, Miriam, who was attending high school at Kenitra Air Base. (This U.S. military base was transferred to the Royal Moroccan Air Force in 1977.)

Marie and Leon were well aware I had dated their son, George. They wished he could come to Morocco for a visit. However, George was in the U.S. Army Reserves and unable to travel abroad. I had hoped that one day I would be part of the Dorros family, and I used these Friday luncheons to get to know them better. I occasionally visited on my own on weekends and even taught Miriam how to drive her parents' white Mustang convertible — quite a head-turner on the streets of Rabat, both the car and the sight of two young females, hair blowing in the wind, out on their own. (Moroccan women our age would be covered head to foot in a long, hooded, baggy robe, called a *djellaba*, and never out without a male family member acting as a chaperone.) Despite my growing closeness with George's family, he and I were still far apart — both geographically and emotionally. At this point, the prospect of marriage seemed rather remote.

During these four years in Morocco, when I was ages 17 to 20, I certainly wasn't going to sit around and wait for a relationship that might never materialize. Besides, Casablanca was a swinging, cosmopolitan city, and its bars and nightclubs beckoned. This was just after the release of the Drifters' version of "On Broadway" (it reached number nine on the Billboard charts in 1963). As soon as the DJ played the opening line, "They say the neon lights are bright on Broadway," people would swarm the dance floor and begin their highly choreographed moves. (This popular line dance was later featured in the opening sequence of the 1979 film *All That Jazz*.) My friends, mostly expats and non-Muslim Moroccans, and I could dance "On Broadway" and others popular in the 1960s, like the Twist and the Watusi, for hours — and did. When we weren't dancing in nightclubs, we were sitting in bars drinking and playing a Yahtzee-like dice game with high stakes. Often, I returned home at dawn, just in time to shower and get dressed to go to work. While I studied really hard at college, these vacations were a time for me to let my hair down, literally, and chill.

On the patio of Villa Mirador, summer 1964

My parents and I would occasionally spend time together during the day on Saturdays (the second day of the Moroccan weekend). We would pack up our station wagon — our personal car as opposed to our official black sedan — with a folding table and beach chairs, a small barbecue grill, and lots of food and beer. My mother would have marinated beef skewers in bourbon (who knows where she got that recipe!) and made French-style potato salad and other dishes. On the beach road, we would buy corn on the cob that had been boiled in salt water from the ocean and then grilled still in the husk. If I close my eyes, I can still smell that corn. We would spend several hours relaxing on one of the most beautiful beaches in the world, eating and drinking, napping and swimming, before heading home so they could get ready for their next round of diplomatic functions.

We also traveled together from time to time. On one trip, we visited Marrakesh, a former imperial city southeast of Casablanca, sometimes called "The Jewel of the South" or the "Red City" because of the color of its red clay buildings. We stayed at the La Mamounia hotel, known for its many famous guests, including Winston Churchill, Nelson Mandela, and Tom Cruise. The hotel was gorgeous, but its gardens containing 700 orange trees and 200 olive trees impressed me the most. We strolled around the *souk*, window-shopping and drinking mint tea whenever merchants offered it. My mother was obsessed with the blue and white ceramics; she had her eye on them for our summer cottage in Gloucester. Later, on another trip to Marrakesh with a friend over Christmas break, we skied in the High Atlas outside of Marrakesh. The ski lifts and trails didn't match Switzerland's, but we had magnificent views of the city and its orange trees below. Plus, I loved to brag that I had skied and then swum in the Atlantic Ocean in a single day!

The summer after my freshman year in college (1964), I sailed from New York with my roommate, Ceci Moore, to Italy on the *United States*, one of the fastest ocean liners in the world — not that we were in any hurry to end the nonstop dining and entertainment, including Broadway shows and deck parties. When we landed in Naples, I was so happy to be back in my old stomping grounds. We traveled around Italy by train armed with the book *Europe on 5 Dollars a Day*, and I proudly showed her Rome and Florence and other places I loved. We parted ways in Florence, and I rode a train for more than 20 hours along the Italian and French Rivieras to Barcelona, where I met up with my parents who had been vacationing on the Costa del Sol on the southeastern coast of Spain.

My parents and I drove back to Casablanca, with stops that included Zaragoza, Guadalajara, Madrid, Toledo, Cordoba, Seville, Cadiz, and Gibraltar. We traveled at a leisurely pace, stopping early enough in the day to sightsee before unwinding at our hotel pool, when there was one, and then heading out late, around 10:00 p.m., for dinner in true Spanish style. We ate fabulous dinners and drank local wines and soaked in the culture at each of our stops, such as spending the better part of two days at the Prado Museum in Madrid. As we traveled south, the Moorish influence became more and more pronounced, so it almost seemed at times like we were already back in Morocco. Until we reached Gibraltar, that is, a very small British enclave known primarily for its nearly 1,400-foot-high Rock of Gibraltar. It was the first time in more than a month I had heard people around me speaking English and even longer since I had partaken in a high tea. We didn't stay long in Gibraltar, soon boarding a car ferry for the 1.5-hour trip to Tangier, at the top tip of Morocco and known historically as a center for spying and smuggling. From Tangier, we drove back to Casablanca, a distance of a little more than 200 miles.

This two-week trip was the longest I have ever spent alone with my parents. It was an opportunity for us to get to know each other better and to begin to establish a new kind of relationship — one in which I was accepted more as a friend than a child. The evolution of our relationship didn't happen overnight. Indeed, many times in Casablanca we reverted to our old, familiar patterns, with my mother raging at me, as she had during the bikini incident in Accra. On one occasion, I had arrived in Casablanca before they returned from home leave. While they were away, my father's beloved cat, Puss-Puss, had produced a litter of five kittens. When I reported this to my mother by phone, she told me to get rid of the kittens by drowning them. I couldn't bring myself to do this, so I gave them to Haj to take them to the pet market. When my mother arrived home, she was livid. "How could you have been so stupid?" she asked over and over again. "You should have kept one kitten to suckle Puss-Puss while her milk dried up," she explained. My "stupidity" led to a painful abscessed mammary gland and a round of antibiotics for the poor mother cat. In my defense, I had no experience with cats — my father had adopted Puss-Puss after I left home — and certainly not with lactating ones. But my mother's words about my stupidity stung, as they had throughout my childhood.

While there were distressing moments like this one, for the most part, my time in Casablanca was positive. I reveled in the respect I garnered through my job at the General Tire & Rubber Company and from my Jewish Moroccan friends, who entrusted me to carry their gold jewelry to relatives in the States for safekeeping. I appreciated our geographic proximity to Europe and the opportunity to travel to places like Spain that were previously unknown to me. The years from age 17 to 20 are generally considered to be maturing ones, and they certainly were for me. When I left Morocco after my spring break in 1967, what was to be my last visit, I was a different person, just months shy of graduating from college. I had spent an academic year, my junior year abroad, studying in Geneva at the African Institute and the Institute of Higher International Studies, focusing on African and Islamic studies. I was no longer the naïve teenager who, on arriving in Casablanca, didn't know the meaning of *haj*. I had a new understanding of Muslims and their culture, which helped me immensely on my later travels to countries like Malaysia, Bangladesh, Pakistan, Brunei, and Indonesia. But my journey from Morocco to Malaysia, the next Muslim country where I would live briefly, was circuitous. It would entail a nearly five-year life-transforming hiatus back in America first.

Homeward Bound

Temporarily (1963 – 1972)

When I was still in elementary school, my parents' friends used to ask me, "Where are you planning to go to college?" I thought it was a strange question. It seemed so remote —at least 10 years away — and I really didn't know much about college. It left me a bit tongue-tied. Before I could formulate an answer, they would always say, "I bet you'll go to Vassar like your grandmother and mother." As the years went on, college and Vassar became synonymous to me. This was further cemented when my sister Eleanor left to attend Vassar after we returned from the Belgian Congo.

When the time finally came for me to apply to colleges, I was living in Rome with access to just one shelf of brochures and booklets, mostly for Catholic colleges in the U.S. and Europe, with a semi-cloistered nun as my college advisor. In my letters to my parents, I toyed with the idea of staying in Europe or going to another "Seven Sisters" college (a favorite aunt, my father's sister Dorothy, had attended Smith, and I was smitten by the Wellesley campus when I visited there with my great aunt Katie, who lived nearby). However, my mother was adamant: I would apply only to Vassar and Sarah Lawrence College. I had never heard of Sarah Lawrence, but my parents had met and were duly impressed by its International Relations professor, Dr. Adda Bozeman, when she traveled to Ghana for research one summer.

The rejection letter from Vassar was profusely apologetic. The admission director was "genuinely distressed" to disappoint the granddaughter, daughter, and sister of alumnae. I had not done well enough on my SAT tests, not surprising since I had never taken a multiple-choice test in my life. At the time, Sarah Lawrence was the only American college that didn't require SAT scores, only a writing sample, so I was admitted based on it and my top ranking in my high school graduating class. It was a poor choice for me. I was coming from a small Catholic high school in Italy to an extremely liberal, avant-garde college just outside of New York City, one of the most expensive colleges in the U.S. — then and now. Its students were predominately Jewish, conspicuously rich, and unbelievably smart. I had won the gold medal in science for chemistry in high school but was left in the dust by the Bronx High School of Science graduates who were in my freshman lab. Moreover, I was used to a traditional curriculum. Sarah Lawrence was based on the Oxford/Cambridge model of one-on-one student-faculty tutorials and independent study, with an emphasis on the performing arts. The biggest shock was that there were no grades, no way of knowing how I was faring academically.

My faculty advisor, called a "don," had no experience with students coming from abroad. Today, it might have been different: both he, Curtis Harnack, and his wife, Hortense Calisher, were writers whose books might now be on my nightstand. It's too bad he never encouraged me; on the contrary, he continuously put me down and, based on the papers I wrote for his English class, said I would never be a writer. It is true I never became a fiction writer, but I did depend on my nonfiction writing for the 50 years of my career. I didn't like Sarah Lawrence or its students — except my roommates, Ceci Moore and Christiane Corbat — or being in the suburbs of New York City. Moreover, these were unsettled times, with nationwide protests against the Vietnam War and race riots in different cities.

President Kennedy was assassinated in the fall of my freshman year. The country was unsettled, and I was even more so. I felt like a fish out of water — academically and socially. My only happy year at college was my junior year abroad, which ironically, I spent back in Europe — in Geneva.

When I first arrived at Sarah Lawrence, the college had overfilled the capacity of the freshman class and was forced to turn some of the double dorm rooms into triples and quadruples. I was placed in one of the quadruple rooms with three other freshmen, one of whom was a harpist who kept her harp in an enormous case in the middle of the room. The situation was untenable; there wasn't space to turn around, much less to unpack my meager belongings. I was told there was nothing the people in charge of housing could do until someone dropped out. Eventually, someone did, and I was able to move into a double room with a sophomore, Caroline (Ceci) Moore, a cultured New Englander whose family lived in Brookline, Massachusetts. I appreciated living with someone who knew her way around — literally and figuratively — and could show me the ropes. The only drawback was that Ceci had an abnormally fast metabolism, and she ate almost constantly; she had a cupboard and a dorm fridge full of food to munch on in between our regular meals in the cafeteria. For me, the results were disastrous: I put on the proverbial "freshman 15" in three months (shades of Rome two years before).

During my sophomore and senior years (before and after my year in Geneva), I lived in the French House, an off-campus house owned by the college. Everyone living there was required to speak exclusively in French. The 12 of us living in the house were all fluent in French, and my roommate, Christiane Corbat, a Swiss-American, was bilingual. (I had lived in two French-speaking African countries and continued to study the language in both high school and college.) Christiane's parents, who lived in a beautiful home on the Long Island Sound in Stamford, Connecticut, took me under their wing. They welcomed me on holidays, like Thanksgiving, when I couldn't go home to Casablanca, and often included me when they came to Bronxville to take Christiane out to dinner. Her Swiss grandmother, who lived in the penthouse apartment of the luxurious Richemond Hotel in Geneva, was equally gracious to me when I was studying there. She would take me by taxi to her favorite restaurant, the five-star Auberge du Père Bise in Talloires, near the Annecy Lake some 25 miles from Geneva, and have the driver wait, meter ticking, while we ate! The Corbats became yet another surrogate family to replace my physically and emotionally absent parents.

Christiane at Sarah Lawrence College

It's impossible to say why Christiane and I became friends in college and remained friends for more than four decades until her untimely death in 2006. Christiane, like many Sarah Lawrence students, was in the arts, an artist experimenting with watercolors, oils, and mixed media. She was dazzled by Joseph Campbell and his courses in comparative mythology and was lightyears away from my more worldly courses in international relations. We had little in common, and she vehemently disapproved of my friends (male and female alike), my religious beliefs, my drinking, and above all, my smoking. In retrospect, I wish I would have listened to her rantings about my smoking. My clothes and hair must have reeked with smoke, but of course, I was oblivious then, as smokers always are. Alas, it would be years before I finally gave up smoking. Christiane and I were constantly at odds, but somehow these differences didn't shatter our bond. I could never have imagined in college what an important role Christiane would play later in my life.

Despite Christiane's disapproval, every Sunday morning, I dragged myself out of bed to go to mass at I Church of St. Joseph, the only Roman Catholic church in the Village of Bronxville. In all the years I went there, no one ever greeted or welcomed me. On the contrary, the congregants used to scowl at me, making clear their distaste for me as a Sarah Lawrence student. The local residents were obviously put out by having a hotbed of liberal education in the middle of their conservative, suburban community. Who could blame them? We were seen as long-haired, jeans-wearing, pot-smoking, tree-hugging, bra-burning, war-protesting hippies. (This was when jeans were a symbol of rebellion, not a ubiquitous fashion choice of the masses.) The SLC girls jammed the local bars and restaurants, generally making a nuisance of themselves. Even though I wore my Sunday best to church (and didn't smoke pot), I was tagged as one of them.

As I didn't feel welcome in Bronxville, I ended up taking my instruction to convert to Catholicism from a Jesuit theologian at Fordham University in the Bronx rather than from the local parish priest. My official conversion took place at Marymount College in Tarrytown, New York, about 25 miles away on the eastern shore of the Hudson River, where my former high school roommate Ann Miller was studying. She was my only Catholic friend living nearby and the only one willing to witness for me. My family wanted nothing to do with it: my father was staunchly anti-Catholic, and the rest seemed uninterested in my decision to leave our Episcopal faith. Once again, I felt very much alone and disconnected from my family.

I was disconnected from even my grandmother Elsie, who had been so supportive of me when I was growing up. She had suddenly become demented in 1959 and had been institutionalized, first in Connecticut near her brother and later in suburban Maryland near my parents. She was diagnosed with atherosclerosis, a hardening of the arteries; in her case, it was the arteries leading to her brain. This may explain why she had inner-ear problems and couldn't travel by plane, as well as her bouts of forgetfulness. I visited her whenever I could, but it wasn't easy for me to get from New York to the Maryland suburbs, especially after my parents moved back overseas, as I didn't have a car. In the beginning, she recognized me, but as the years went by, she no longer knew who I was. I eventually stopped going because the nurses said my visits upset her. They upset me, too. It was too much for me to see this formerly intelligent and interesting woman, whom I loved and admired, reduced to a mere shadow of herself. The only saving grace was that, by losing her mind, she was able to erase much of her difficult past and 67-year widowhood.

Me at Sarah Lawrence College

When I studied at Sarah Lawrence, it was all female and had, what seemed to me, a large number of lesbians. It didn't officially become coeducational until the year after I graduated, although there was one lone male on campus during my time there. (Even today, it's predominately female, with about 400 males and 1,000 females). In order to meet men, my heterosexual classmates and I went to mixers at nearby colleges, like Columbia or NYU, or even weekend gatherings at colleges farther afield, like Yale, Brown, and Williams. I thoroughly enjoyed meeting all these young men, and we always had a good time at these parties — lots of drinking and dancing, especially to the ever-popular Beatles music.

During these years, I had an on-again, off-again relationship with George. We had reconnected in December 1962 when I came back to the States for my sister Kathy's wedding; at the time, I was a senior at Marymount High School in Rome, and he was a freshman at Duke University. Once I was in college, we saw each other on rare occasions, usually in Washington, D.C. However, I had more in common with him than I did with most of the young men I was meeting at college mixers. George and I had known each other since we were teenagers and shared similar experiences and values. We had both grown up as Foreign Service "brats," loved travel and adventure, were liberal Democrats, and, once I converted to Catholicism, also belonged to the same faith. We could talk for hours — and often did when we were together — and felt very comfortable in each other's company, like best friends, but with a strong physical attraction.

George and I had fallen in love in Rome, one of the most romantic places on earth. We fell in love all over again in New York City during my senior year in college. We spent a glorious weekend in the Big Apple in early December 1966, doing all the things that made the city the perfect backdrop for popular rom-com movies, like *An Affair to Remember, Breakfast at Tiffany's,* and *Moonstruck.* We went to the top of the Empire State Building, rode the Staten Island Ferry at sunset, and took a horse-drawn carriage around Central Park. The soundtrack to our rekindled relationship was the theme song of the French movie *Un homme et une femme (A Man and a Woman),* which had recently been released in the States. We watched the award-winning movie together, holding hands, connecting to both the love story in the movie and to each other. I can't explain why we related so completely with the couple in that movie; they were French, older, widow and widower, both with young children. But their romance touched us and stoked the embers of our relationship that had nearly burned out after our breakup in Rome and subsequent years of geographic separation. After watching the movie, we walked to

Rockefeller Center and admired the gigantic Christmas tree — that year a 64-foot Canadian spruce decorated with nearly 20,000 lights. We ice skated at the iconic outdoor rink and then sat at an adjacent bar to have a warming cocktail. In those days, my drink of choice was Dubonnet, a French wine-based aperitif, which complemented the movie and the festive holiday atmosphere of Rockefeller Center.

With George (undated)

While George and I had fallen back in love and were contemplating marriage, we wouldn't become formally engaged for another year. In the meantime, we pursued a long-distance relationship as I finished up my last year of college and George began working in Northern Virginia, outside of Washington, D.C. He was no longer a student (he left Duke in the middle of his junior year), so he had joined the U.S. Army Reserves to avoid being drafted. He visited my college campus a few times, for example, on his way back from active duty at Fort Devens, Massachusetts. He was welcomed by a handful of my friends but not by most of the students. This was close to the height of the Vietnam War, and Sarah Lawrence College students were mostly staunch anti-war activists; to them, George, with his buzz cut and Army uniform, represented the worst of the military establishment. (He would go on to serve one weekend a month and two weeks a year until he had completed his six-year commitment to the Army in 1971.) We considered living together, but we didn't want to face the disapproval of our parents. We decided to continue to pursue our separate lives until such time as we could finally get married.

With my parents, graduation from Sarah Lawrence College, June 1967

After I graduated from Sarah Lawrence with a degree in international relations, I moved to Boston to work for the father of a classmate of mine at the Children's Hospital there. It was technically a secretarial position, but my boss, Dr. Thomas Cone Jr. gave me a number of important projects, including reviewing books and manuscripts for *The Journal of Pediatrics* (he was then the editor-in-chief). I rented a one-bedroom apartment near Fenway Park, across from the Museum of Fine Arts and walking distance to work and neighborhood stores and restaurants. It was the first time I had lived by myself, after years of roommates in high school and college, and I relished every minute of it. I was occasionally lonely, but I loved my job and my new friends and, above all, my independence and the chance to explore all that Boston had to offer. On warm summer evenings, I could hear the roar of Red Sox fans at Fenway Park through my open windows, but regrettably, I never attended a game. I was too busy doing other things. My life was both filled full and fulfilled. In retrospect, I should have stayed longer than a year; my time there seemed very short.

At Christmas that year (1967), George and I met up to spend the holidays with my parents in Chevy Chase. They had returned to their home on Bradley Lane after their last overseas assignment in Casablanca. As was the Green family tradition, we ate a seafood meal on Christmas Eve, lit the candles on the tree (yes, actual candles, not lights!), sang a few carols, and put the presents under the tree. George retrieved an enormous box from his car; it was gift-wrapped and had my name on it. I couldn't imagine what he might have gotten for me. I had knitted him a sweater. When we opened our presents on Christmas morning, I left George's for last. I opened the box, only to find another smaller box inside, and then another, and another. At last, I reached a small jewelry box. Much to my surprise, it contained an engagement ring. (Now I realize this was the second time I was given a diamond ring on Christmas day!) We hadn't discussed the timing of our engagement, and I don't remember if George had asked my father for my hand in marriage, but I was ecstatic. I felt like I was in a musical, and at any moment, I would burst into song. Our Christmas breakfast was accompanied by Champagne toasts; we must have all been a bit tipsy in church later that morning. I returned to Boston and spent a ridiculous amount of time during the next eight months in long-distance wedding preparations.

Wedding day, Chevy Chase, August 31, 1968

We were married over Labor Day weekend in 1968, at relatively young ages by today's standards, but at that time, the average age for a man to marry was 23.1 years and 20.8 for a woman; George was turning 25, and I was 22. That year was one of the most tumultuous years in U.S. history, marked by the civil rights movement, shocking assassinations — Martin Luther King Jr. in April and Robert Kennedy in June — and massive protests against the Vietnam War. George had to get special dispensation to be present at our wedding: his Army Reserve unit had been mobilized to deploy to Chicago where the Youth International Party (Yippies) were trying to nominate a pig, Pigasus the Immortal, at the Democratic National Convention, held August 26 to 29, just days before our wedding on the 31st.

Once again, the country was unsettled, and I felt even more so. My mother had commandeered our wedding from start to finish. I had wanted a small wedding with just family and friends, about 35 people in all. Instead, we ended up with 10 times as many, 350 at both the church and the reception, mostly friends of my parents whom I had never met and would never see again. Worse, when asked by guests what we wanted as a wedding present, she told them silver. We ended up with silver flatware, silver serving dishes, silver trays, silver picture frames, and just about anything else that could be made out of silver, even silver salt and pepper shakers. What we really needed was a toaster and other mundane kitchen appliances.

Around this time, women's liberation organizations had been formed in major cities, and feminism was on the rise. The first few years of our marriage were fraught with the tensions created by the changes in gender roles. These were complicated by the fact that I was the principal breadwinner during the years George was finishing his B.A. and MBA degrees at American University (in 1969 and 1971, respectively). Even though I was working full-time and George was at home studying, he wouldn't deign to push the vacuum cleaner around or put in a load of laundry. His family was aghast that he would be financially dependent on me. It was something out of *My Big Fat Greek Wedding*, except in our case, the groom was Greek, and my family was the White Anglo-Saxon Protestant one. Our cultural differences, coupled with our personality differences (we later scored completely opposite on the Myers-Briggs Type Indicator test), led to some major conflicts and misunderstandings. But by and large, we were happy, although I was exhausted all the time.

I had started working at the liaison office of the European Union in Washington, D.C., a week before I got married. (The fact they couldn't wait for me to start until I got back from our one-week honeymoon in the Outer Banks of North Carolina should have been a red flag.) At that time, it was called the European Economic Community (EEC) and consisted of only six countries — France, West Germany, Italy, and the three Benelux countries: Belgium, the

Netherlands, and Luxembourg. (With the withdrawal of the United Kingdom in 2020, there are currently 27 members.)

The office had one representative from each of the six countries, and partly because I was fluent in French, I was assigned to the French representative, Pierre Malvé, a workaholic and demanding boss if ever there was one. Once, I had to go into the office late on a Saturday between the wedding and reception of my sister-in-law, Miriam, because he didn't like the way he signed his name on the letters I had left for him. I often worked until midnight (6:00 a.m. in Brussels), telexing reports to the EEC headquarters before their offices opened in the morning. (Sending a telex was a time-consuming and cumbersome process that involved typing holes in a long, thin strip of paper tape, about a half inch wide, and then threading the tape through a machine that "read" the holes and transmitted the message.) Despite the primitive technology, I enjoyed the work, which included, among other things, attending Congressional hearings on Capitol Hill whenever European trade was discussed.

I had thought I might want to be a teacher (a good profession for a woman in those days), so I was also taking courses for a master's degree in education at George Washington University a couple of nights a week when I could get away early enough from work. On the weekends, I had to study in addition to grocery shopping, cleaning our apartment, cooking and freezing meals for the week, doing laundry, and ironing George's Army uniforms when he was going to serve as a weekend warrior. If we took a drive on a Sunday afternoon, I invariably fell asleep in the passenger seat. Despite the busyness and my constant fatigue, we dreamed of starting a family.

On a gorgeous day in late spring 1971, I was brimming with joy and new life — literally. I was at the 12-week mark of my first pregnancy, starting my second trimester, when common wisdom said it was "safe" to divulge the news. Until then, it was all we could do not to tell our family and friends — we were both so excited about our first child-to-be. However, we knew well the statistics on early miscarriages and didn't want to jump the gun. Even though I was not yet showing and had yet to experience any fetal movement, I felt like my slowly growing uterus was the center of the universe. I was living in Arlington, Virginia, just across the Potomac River from Washington, D.C. I dialed the number I knew by heart to my childhood home. "Hello, Mother," I gushed. "I have some exciting news." (Growing up, all my friends called their mothers "Mom" or even "Mommy," but mine had always been the old-fashioned and slightly stilted "Mother.")

There was a brief pause and then my mother said, "And I have news for you." Without waiting for me to respond, she explained that the day before she had been given the diagnosis of advanced colorectal cancer. After what seemed like an interminable discussion of upcoming treatments, including surgery and chemotherapy, she finally remembered that it was her youngest daughter on the other end of the phone, and I had news to share. By then, I was totally deflated, as if all the air had gone out of my body. The joy was gone. All I could feel was incredible sadness and a smidgen of anger that she had, once again, stolen the spotlight. "I'm going to have a baby," I reported in a flat monotone, not knowing if she would be alive in November to welcome him or her into the world. It seemed so very cruel that I had a dark cloud hanging over one of the most beautiful days of my life.

The other dark cloud hanging over us at that time was George's career prospects. Our fathers had spent the better part of their careers working for the U.S. Department of State, with home base in Washington, D.C., peppered with assignments abroad, mostly in Africa. (George's father had six foreign assignments, mine had three.) George and I both appreciated growing up overseas. We decided that the international life was for us, but in the corporate environment, not the diplomatic one. George had just graduated with an MBA, majoring in international business, and had begun applying to American corporations and banks with overseas operations. He traveled to New York and other places for interviews. However, this was the summer of 1971. The U.S. economy had tanked and was in a major recession marked by energy shortages, high inflation, and high unemployment. Months went by without George getting as much as a nibble, much less an offer.

We were beginning to get desperate. My pregnancy was progressing: I was due in late November/early December. I had quit my job with the liaison office of the European Union, where I had worked for four years, and we had relinquished our apartment, thinking we would be moving soon. If I had known how bad the recession was going to be, I wouldn't have done either. I ended up having to work temp jobs to make ends meet. While George was on the road job hunting, I stayed with my parents at their summer cottage in Gloucester. There I worked as a medical transcriber at the local health center. I had medical experience from working at Children's Hospital in Boston right out of college, plus I knew Latin and could type, all very handy skills when transcribing records on the world's original word processor. Once again, the technology was primitive and cumbersome, but for the first time ever, the notes in a patient's file were neatly typed instead of scribbled in the doctor's often illegible handwriting.

At the end of the summer, I moved back to Washington, D.C., and found temporary work with the League of Women Voters. I was not living my dream, to put it mildly. After four years of financially stable, independent married life, here I was — 25 years old, pregnant, and living with my husband and his parents in their cramped two-bedroom apartment. I was anxious about our future, which I knew wasn't good for my unborn baby, but in those days, holistic practices, like mindfulness and meditation, weren't yet in the mainstream. I walked a lot and worked out at the gym, and my mother-in-law prepared healthy meals for me, so at least physically I was in good shape.

I was still at work when my labor began. As the contractions were mild, I took my time going home to take a long, leisurely shower, eat a light snack, and grab my labor bag before heading to Sibley Memorial Hospital, only a couple of miles from my in-laws' apartment in Northwest Washington, D.C. I thought I was prepared for labor and delivery: I had read tons of books and taken Lamaze classes with George. But nothing could have prepared me for the agony of labor that lasted more than 12 hours. I began to regret my decision to have a "natural" labor and delivery. As labor intensified, I would have given just about anything to have an epidural. But we hung in there, with George applying pressure to counteract my back pain and offering me ice chips along with words of encouragement. George had bought a new camera to take pictures, but he hardly had time, especially when our baby's heart rate dropped and the doctor thought I might need a cesarean section (thankfully, I didn't).

Our son, Gregory Leon, was finally born at 4:56 a.m. Tears streamed down our cheeks as we held our newborn and watched the dawning of a new day — literally and figuratively. George and I were both overwhelmed by emotions, primarily joy at the birth of our first child but also apprehension about being new parents. Greg was not a pretty sight: he had emerged in face presentation, entering the birth canal face first, so his head and face were badly misshapen and bruised. His eyes were swollen to just slits, giving him the look of the cartoon character Mister Magoo (a nickname that stuck for the first couple of weeks of his life). Fortunately, the swelling and bruising slowly dissipated, and his eyes morphed from slits into large, round blue eyes. Everyone said the color of his eyes would change as he got older, but they never did. He inherited the recessive blond hair, blue-eyed genes of ancestors on both sides of the family. My health insurance had a rider that excluded maternity care, so I spent only the mandatory 24 hours in the hospital in order not to rack up bills we couldn't afford to pay.

Now that we had a child, the fact that neither George nor I was gainfully employed (and I had no paid maternity leave) kept us awake at night, along with our screaming newborn. Given our growing level of desperation, it's not surprising that George jumped at his first job offer. It came as a telegram from the World Health Organization (WHO) asking if he could report to work at its headquarters in Geneva on January 1, 1972, less than a month away, for a temporary assignment. (George had done some part-time work at the Pan American Health Organization in Washington, D.C., while he was working on his MBA and had some contacts in the system.) We were giddy with excitement: George finally had a full-time job offer, and we were headed back overseas.

From Home to Away

As George was hired as a consultant, WHO was not going to pay for infant Greg or me to accompany him. However, I wasn't about to sit in the States while George went off to Geneva (shades of my mother when she insisted on accompanying my father to Paris in 1951). Greg was only three weeks old when I rushed to get him a passport, trying to hold up his head for his photo without my hands showing. We packed our suitcases with warm clothing for the winter weather in Switzerland, only to find out the day after we arrived in Geneva that George was to do a series of two-month consultancies, first in Singapore and then in Malaysia. We felt like the rug had been pulled out from under us. It had been, but then telegrams don't leave much room for nuance.

I sent a telegram to my mother and asked her to airfreight us a suitcase of summer clothes. We had left all our earthly belongings in my parents' attic in Chevy Chase. Then I purchased another youth fare ticket (I had not yet turned 26), this time a roundtrip ticket from London to Singapore out of our meager savings. It's one of the best decisions I've ever made. I had never been to Asia before, and the stays in Singapore and Malaysia opened my eyes to a whole new world.

We lucked out in Singapore: after just a few days staying in a hotel room, we were able to sublet a house from a British couple who were going on an extended home leave. The house was completely furnished and came with a maid, gardener, and *amah* (nanny), as well as the use of their car. It took me a while to get used to driving their stick shift Mini Cooper on the left side of the road (and changing gears with my left hand), but once I mastered it, I was off. I put more than 2,000 miles on the car in two months on an island that is only 279 square miles.

Singapore is a study in contrasts, ranging from the sleek, ultramodern skyscrapers to the crowded, squalid squatter settlements (later bulldozed to make way for sprawling housing estates); from the concrete overpasses to the lush green parks; and from the noisy, bustling quays along the river to the tranquil residential areas. I explored every nook and cranny of this island city-state, visiting markets and national treasures, and becoming immersed in Chinese culture — the food, the art, the calligraphy. In between jaunts, I went back to the house to breastfeed Greg and take him out for walks in our neighborhood. Despite all the restrictions (e.g., fines for chewing gum and public floggings for minor transgressions), I felt very free in Singapore.

Our *amah*, who grew very fond of us, asked us to a number of her family gatherings, including the wedding of one of her relatives. The wedding produced some surprises — the bride wore bright red, we ate glutinous rice balls ("tangyuan," symbolizing being together with your beloved), red envelopes stuffed with cash were *de rigueur* as gifts for the newlyweds, and the men guzzled expensive brandy as if it were water. (This was my first time witnessing the inability of some Asians to metabolize alcohol, known as aldehyde dehydrogenase deficiency, resulting in glassy eyes, extreme flushing of the face, and rapid drunkenness. I would see a lot of it in my subsequent years in Asia, especially in the Philippines and China.) We were not in Singapore for long, but in two short months, we experienced more local culture than most expatriates did in years.

Malaysia was just across a causeway from Singapore, but we had never been there. (The insurance on our car was only valid in Singapore and, since we knew we would be living there soon, hadn't bothered to visit.) When the time came for us to relocate to Kuala Lumpur, we went by train, a trip that took a little more than six hours. Kuala Lumpur, or KL as it is known, was very different from Singapore. It was on the small size for Asia — about a half million people — and totally chaotic compared to the regulated life of Singaporeans. The streets were clogged with animal-drawn carts, motorcycles, imported cars, honking taxis, and belching, overfilled buses. The city, like the entire country, was a mishmash of native Malays (about 50%), Chinese (23%), and Indians (7%), with the rest made up of other native groups and foreigners, mostly British who had stayed on after the colony's independence in 1957.

We lived in a lovely bungalow next to the National Museum and the Lake Gardens, a sprawling park with tree-lined walking trails, botanical gardens, and a planetarium. We were awakened every morning at dawn to the sound of the muezzin's call to prayer (Malaysians are predominately Muslim), birdsong, and a soft knock on our door to indicate that our breakfast was waiting for us on our front porch. We ate the rest of our meals in a communal dining room with the other transient expatriates. The food on a fixed daily menu was mostly British, like shepherd's pie, and Indian; mutton curry was a weekly regular.

I was thrilled to have another two-month break from cooking, housework, and laundry. I didn't careen around as much as I had in Singapore since I didn't have a nanny and Greg would only handle so many outings in one day. However, on weekends, we traveled around the Malaysian countryside and went to a handful of the country's 800-plus islands and beaches. Our favorite getaways were the hill resorts, like Fraser's Hill and the Cameron Highlands. These Raj-style hill resorts, called stations, offered a relatively cool climate and a respite from the bustle of the capital city. All in all, it was a very interesting, mostly stress-free, and culturally enriching stay.

George was then supposed to go off on a third two-month assignment, this time in Kenya. We were excited about the prospect of returning to Africa, but the timing didn't seem right. It was difficult living out of suitcases with an infant, especially since this was before disposable diapers were available in much of the world. Since George had proved himself during his first two assignments, he asked for something more permanent. WHO offered him a position in either its Regional Office for South-East Asia in New Delhi or its Regional Office for the Western Pacific in Manila. Not knowing much about either place, we flipped a coin and ended up choosing Manila. (More than four decades later, when I finally visited New Delhi for the first time, I realized we had made the right decision.)

It would have been easy if we could have flown directly from Kuala Lumpur to Manila; the flight takes only a few hours. Instead, we went all the way around the world in the other direction — Asia to Europe, Europe to the States, and the States back to Asia via the Pacific route. George had to go back to Geneva for briefings, and I had my return ticket to London. While I was in the U.K., I took the opportunity to visit my sister Eleanor, who was doing her Ph.D. in English literature at the University of Nottingham. I then went back to Chevy Chase to pack up all our earthly belongings to ship to the Philippines. We went to Gloucester for a brief vacation to visit my parents and to say goodbye again. The timing was fortuitous since my mother was back in the hospital battling her colorectal cancer. Her spirits were buoyed immensely by seeing her grandson, Greg, now eight months old, and by the chocolate milkshakes we snuck in for her.

While we were in Gloucester, the weather was unusually stormy, and the waves crashed on the rocks in front of our family cottage. We learned it was from the vestiges of Hurricane Agnes that had clobbered the mid-Atlantic states (end of June – beginning of July 1972). We didn't think much about it until we were informed by our moving company that the plywood crate containing all our belongings was sitting under several feet of water in Baltimore harbor; it hadn't been loaded onto the boat going to Manila before the hurricane struck. Everything was ruined — our wedding photos and presents (all that silver!), Moroccan rugs, Congolese ivory statues, lamps, paintings, clothing, kitchenware, appliances, a new stereo system still in its original box, linens, yearbooks, memorabilia, and toys for Greg. The flooding at the docks was deemed "an act of God," so we received no insurance payment for our loss. We set out for our new life in Manila with little more than the clothes on our backs.

Obligatory Stopover

George left for Manila before I did to start his new job and look for a place for us to live. When it was my time to leave, my mother suddenly became uncharacteristically concerned about me traveling halfway around the world with a colicky infant. She had never seemed to worry about me when I traveled alone before, not even when I was 15 and left for boarding school. I was now 25, and her concern seemed too late and unreasonable. Perhaps her battle with cancer was making her feel vulnerable, and she was transferring that vulnerability to me.

In the absence of anyone to accompany me to the Philippines, she insisted I stop on the way and stay with her relatives in Honolulu, Barbara and Joe Pynchon. Barbara was my mother's first cousin. (Many knew Barbara by her nickname, Bunny, but I always called her by her given name.) Barbara had married young, had two children, and then gotten divorced, something that was frowned upon in the 1950s. When she got remarried to Joe Pynchon, they decided to leave New England and move as far away as they could from disapproving family members. Joe became headmaster of La Pietra Hawaii School for Girls, a school he helped found in 1964. He served as head of the school until he retired in 1991 — nearly three decades later. Because the Pynchons had moved away when I was young, I had never met them. I had only met Barbara's daughter, Anne, when we spent one Thanksgiving together with her grandmother (my great aunt Katie), when Anne and I were both in college. I was hesitant to descend upon the Pynchons, but it did seem preferable to flying 8,400-plus miles directly to Manila with only fuel stops on the West Coast and in Guam.

Barbara and Joe welcomed me with open arms. Within an hour of my arrival at the airport in Honolulu, I was settled into the guestroom of their lovely home on Royal Circle. Their lanai, where they spent a lot of their family time, overlooked the ocean. I was intoxicated by the scents of the flora around the house — jasmine, plumeria, gardenia, and others I couldn't identify. I sighed in contentment, and even Greg settled down from his cross-country crying jag (pity the people who sat next to us on the plane). Joe barbecued mahi-mahi, and by the time we sat down for dinner, we were no longer strangers but, on our way, to becoming the closest of cousins and lifelong friends.

The Pynchons at home in Honolulu

I was enchanted by Hawaii. Barbara and Joe took us on a tour of Oahu, bypassing the congested shopping areas and stopping for a picnic at one of the remote beaches. With Greg in his baby carrier, we strolled around the campus of the Hawaii School for Girls at the foot of Diamond Head. Joe was justifiably proud of the school he had founded and now ran. The design of the main building of La Pietra was inspired by an Italian villa in Florence by the same name and reminded me of my boarding school in Rome. There was so much to see and do on the island. My visit ended all too quickly, and it was time for Greg and me to continue our journey to Manila. Unfortunately, all the flights to the Philippines left in the middle of the night. Joe sat up with me, and we played Scrabble until it was time for him to drive us back to the airport.

Little did I know then that this would be the beginning of a 14-year tradition. Two years later, I returned to Honolulu, this time with George, and we continued our visits until 1986 — no longer obligatory stopovers but highly desirable ones. Sometimes we stopped on our way from the Philippines to the States and sometimes from the States back to the Philippines. On the latter stopovers, Joe always sat up and played Scrabble with me. To this day, whenever I play Scrabble, I think of Cousin Joe and his quirky rules, like not being able to play the same word twice in a single game. The Pynchons were busy people; during that 14-year period, they had two sons living at home (Barbara's second set of children). Barbara and Joe were actively involved in their sons' activities and the community in which Joe worked. Nonetheless, they always found time to spend some with us when we visited and to make us feel at home. Their house on Royal Circle became a true home away from home. One summer, we arranged a house swap. We stayed in their house in Honolulu while they stayed in ours in Geneva. Our lives became so entwined it is hard to remember a time when they weren't part of mine. Their passing — Joe in 2008 and Barbara in 2009 — left a gigantic hole in my heart. In spite of my grief, I will be forever grateful to my mother for forcing me to make that stopover in Honolulu nearly a half century ago.

Pearl of the Orient

Manila (August 1972 – March 1986)

Part 1: Turbulent Arrival

On Saturday evening, September 23, 1972, George and I went to a performance of Leonard Bernstein's *Mass*. This iconic theater piece for musicians, singers, and dancers had debuted exactly a year earlier for the inauguration of the John F. Kennedy Center for the Performing Arts in Washington, D.C. I had never seen it performed, but I had played my record of it so many times it's a wonder the vinyl still held up! I was particularly excited about this performance because I had just arrived in Manila four weeks earlier and was told that Filipinos were gifted musicians, singers, and dancers, and their version would be even better than the original. As soon as George and I started walking toward the theater, I sensed something was wrong. The entrance was surrounded by Philippine military with machine guns and sniffer dogs. My purse was searched, and I was roughly patted down by a male security guard. Being new to the city, I didn't know if this was standard procedure, but the nervous whispering of the Filipinos around me told me it was not.

The year 1972 was a turbulent one in Philippine history. There had been 20 bombings between March 15 and September 11 in various locations around metro Manila. In retrospect, it was clear that many of the theater goers were fearful that the military might have gotten wind of yet another potential bombing. Some people left, but George and I stayed, oblivious of the risk we were taking. At the beginning of the performance, I was too nervous to enjoy it, but slowly as the familiar, haunting melodies of *Mass* filled the theater, I got carried away and completely forgot my fears. I have seen *Mass* performed a few times since, including by the Los Angeles Philharmonic, but this was by far and away the most brilliant production. The Filipinos brought new and unbridled energy to the already high-octane libretto.

As it turned out, when we arrived at the theater shortly after 7:00 p.m., President Ferdinand Marcos had just announced he had placed the entirety of the Philippines under martial law. (The proclamation was dated two days earlier, September 21, so the military was on high alert, especially for large gatherings.) We went home after the performance and went to bed. Early the next morning, one of George's colleagues arrived at the house in a taxi to tell us martial law had been declared and we should leave the country immediately. We packed a small suitcase for us and our then 10-month-old son, Greg, gathered our passports, and prepared to head to the airport. Before we left, however, we began to have second thoughts. There was no way of knowing what was going to happen next, and we couldn't jeopardize George's first permanent assignment with WHO based on one person's advice. We decided to stick it out. And stick it out we did — from 1972 through the time martial law was formally lifted (January 1981) and until three weeks after Marcos was exiled from the country in February 1986 — for a total of nearly 14 years.

When I had touched down at Manila International Airport in late August, I had heard about the bombings, but I knew next to nothing about the country and its culture. I had borrowed a few books from my local public library and learned the bare outline of its history:

The Philippines were claimed in 1521 by Ferdinand Magellan, a Portuguese explorer sailing for Spain, who named the islands after King Philip II of Spain. After several more incursions, the Spanish ruled the Philippines for 333 years. At the end of the Spanish-American war in 1898, Spain ceded the Philippines, Guam, and Puerto Rico to the United States for $20 million. The U.S. occupied the Philippines for 48 years until independence was declared on the Fourth of July, 1946.

Naively, I weighed 333 years of Spaniards versus 48 years of Americans and assumed I would be going to a country where the people spoke Spanish, danced the flamenco, and ate paella. I wasn't alone: every time I mentioned I was relocating to the Philippines, people asked me if I spoke Spanish (I didn't and still don't). Only one Spanish restaurant in Manila, called Sevilla, served paella and on Saturday nights featured a pair of flamenco dancers, but that was it. Except for the tenacity of the Catholic Church, which continued to influence the country's education system and social mores, the Philippines was much more oriented toward the U.S. than Spain. At its heart, Filipino culture is Indigenous Asian — a mishmash of Malay (95%) and Chinese — with a veneer of Americana. In general, the people are friendly, hospitable, resilient, family oriented, deeply religious, and amazingly artistic, as witnessed by their production of Bernstein's *Mass*.

By the time I arrived in the Philippines, I had lived in eight countries: France, the Belgian Congo, Ghana, Italy, Morocco, Switzerland, Singapore, and Malaysia. And I had traveled to countless more: most of western Europe, including Austria, Belgium, Germany, Liechtenstein, Luxembourg, Monaco, the Netherlands, and the United Kingdom, as well as Canada (summer and winter), Greece, Mexico, and Tunisia for vacations. That I was well-traveled, there was no doubt. Nonetheless, I was anxious. This was my first long-term assignment with my husband and young child. I didn't have my parents or an educational institution to fall back on. I didn't have the support of the U.S. Government to ease my way. Today, with the resources of the internet, it wouldn't seem so daunting to find a place to live and set up a new home. Without even a phone, I was completely overwhelmed.

On our arrival, the Vietnam War was still ongoing, but negotiations had begun in Paris to try to hammer out a peace agreement and a withdrawal strategy for the United States. At the height of the war, the U.S. Embassy in Manila had rented dozens of houses for military advisors and officers on R & R from Vietnam. We were lucky to be able to sublet one of these houses, a sprawling two-story, four-bedroom house with a large garden in Makati, the nicest suburban neighborhood in Manila, for the rock-bottom price of $100 a month. It was fully furnished, and as we had few belongings besides our clothes, we quickly settled in.

George carpooled to work at the WHO office with four colleagues, so all but one day a week, our new Toyota Corona (somewhere between today's Corolla and Camry), imported directly from Japan, was mine. I explored my environs, found the closest stores, and attended meetings of the local American women's club. From these women, I learned everything I needed to know about living in Manila and all the local gossip. I took lessons in bridge and mahjong and whittled away many hours at play. In the evenings, we attended cocktail or dinner parties or entertained at home. We all had plenty of domestic help: at one point, we had a cook, a nanny (*yaya*), a washerwoman (*labandera*), a driver, and a part-time gardener.

One of the women I met early on, Edith Derting, who later became a dear friend, talked me into going horseback riding with her. I had only been on a horse a couple of times in my life, but it quickly became a passion. I went riding almost every day, sometimes out in the fields around the stables, but more often taking lessons in the ring, learning dressage and jumping, and even polo. I wore tailor-made white jodhpurs (which kept the *labandera* busy!) and handmade black leather boots, with an assortment of helmets, velvet riding jackets, and cravats for competitions. I competed in dressage and jumping but had to forgo polo; I didn't own a horse, much less the six needed to change to a fresh mount after each chukker (a period in polo lasting seven and a half minutes). It was a great way to ride:

I could spend as much time as I liked on a horse borrowed from the stable and, when I was done, hand it back to a groom. No brushing, no feeding, no lugging saddles, no mucking. I rode for years until I was four months pregnant with Chris in 1975 and again until I was four months pregnant with Sam in 1980. I haven't been on a horse since — more than four decades later.

Horse jumping competition, 1973

Part 2: Never Stop Learning!

Despite the exorbitant amount of time I spent horseback riding, I was the one chomping at the bit! I certainly wasn't using much brainpower, and I longed to do something intellectual. For my entire life, until the year before, I had always been studying or working. I wasn't used to a life of leisure; my only activities besides horseback riding were playgroups with my young son, mahjong (I gave up bridge early on), and evening engagements with George, when he wasn't traveling. Education beckoned. The University of the Philippines, the best in the country and fully accredited in the U.S., was closed because of martial law. However, it was due to reopen the following January, and I was determined to begin working on a degree. Because I am directionally challenged, it took every ounce of courage I had to drive to the campus in Quezon City to the north of Manila. (This was before I had a driver and long before GPS.) I eventually found the admissions office on the sprawling campus, filled out an application, attached a certified copy of my college transcript, paid my fee, and then drove home to wait and see if I would be accepted. I was. Once I was a bona fide UP student, I chose the Master of Asian Studies program since I was living in Asia and knew very little about the region.

For my degree, I had to learn an Asian language. I considered Tagalog, the national language of the Philippines, which I had begun studying and using conversationally with our domestic help or at the market, but I wasn't that enamored with it. I could have taken the easy way out and used my French and majored in Vietnamese studies, but I was intrigued by the characters in Japanese and Chinese. In the end, I settled on Chinese, initially studying traditional characters in textbooks imported from Taiwan. It wasn't until the Philippines established diplomatic relations with China in 1975 that I switched to simplified characters and the *pinyin* romanization system. We had to learn 10 characters a day, five days a week, until we had memorized the more than 2,000 characters required for our comprehensive exam. I struggled with the language: every time I learned 50 new characters in one week, I forgot some of the 50 I had learned the previous week. Most of the Chinese-Filipinos spoke Cantonese or Fukienese, so I wasn't able to practice my Mandarin with them. I tried to watch Chinese movies, but most were kung fu with lots of grunts or rom-coms with lots of sighs. I could read and write (political slogans like "Long Live Marxism, Leninism and Mao Zedong Thought"), understand a little, but I couldn't converse or read anything practical like a menu by the time I took my first trip to China in 1978.

It took me four years, rather than the standard two, to finish my master's degree. I could only balance a half load of courses with the demands of wifehood and motherhood. I found my courses in pre-modern and modern Asian history fascinating (not so much the required methods courses). I learned so much about a region I had never come across before. While taking classes on China, I was drawn to the role of women in that country, specifically the 1950 Marriage Law. With the passage of this law, women, who had traditionally been subservient to men — to their fathers when young, their husbands when married, and their sons when widowed — were granted equal rights, at least on paper. I immersed myself in research on this topic, spending part of one home leave in the Harvard–Yenching Library in Cambridge, Massachusetts. (The libraries at the University of the Philippines left a lot to be desired: books listed in the card catalogue went missing, and articles were torn out of journals. Had their collections been intact, I would not have had to consult a library halfway around the world.)

When it came to producing six copies of my thesis, "The 1950 Marriage Law of the People's Republic of China: Its Repercussions on the Status of Women in Chinese Society," I hired a temp from Manpower to do the typing. I had found it terribly frustrating typing it myself on an old IBM Selectric typewriter with an original sheet and five onionskin paper copies interspersed with carbon paper. If I made a mistake, I had to correct it with liquid Wite-Out on the original and erase each of the subsequent sheets. Also, the footnotes had to be at the bottom of each page, not at the end of the chapter or the thesis, as is now the norm. The man sat at a card table in our living room for what seemed like forever, pecking away at the keys with undoubtedly little idea of what he was typing. I published some of my thesis research in various journals, such as the *Philippine Law Journal* and the *Philippine Social Sciences and Humanities Review*. I was thus considered a China expert and gave lectures at different universities around Manila, taught courses at UP, and became the editor of *The China Reader*, the newsletter of the Association of Philippine-China Understanding.

I was also auditing courses at the medical school of the University of the Philippines. I had read extensively and taken Lamaze classes when I was pregnant with our first child. This approach to childbirth resonated with me, and I had decided to train to become a Lamaze instructor. To pass the qualifying exam, I needed to take classes in anatomy and physiology, normal and abnormal childbirth, and anesthesiology. There had never been an auditor in the medical school, and my request was met with tough resistance, but I used my connections at WHO and was finally given permission. In addition to a written exam, I had to attend a training workshop in person, available only in the U.S. and Europe. I ended up going to Buffalo, New York (where I first ate buffalo wings!), to attend one that fit my schedule. I started teaching series of six weekly classes to pregnant women and their labor coach, usually their husband but sometimes a relative or friend. But first I had to work with the obstetricians and hospitals to allow a labor coach, dubbed a "companion," in the labor and deliver rooms. Most hospitals had rules against it. I gave lectures at medical conferences, was interviewed on national television, and met one-on-one with prominent obstetricians. Some balked at the most innovative ideas — underwater births, piped-in music, beanbags, and birthing chairs — but many came around to accepting the less threatening aspects of Lamaze. In effect, I singlehandedly created a mini-revolution in childbirth in Manila that eventually spread to other parts of the Philippines. I consider it one of my top lifetime achievements.

I ended up teaching 64 series of classes, with a total of more than 1,000 students — classes that included information not only on labor and delivery but also prenatal exercise and breastfeeding, as well as a tour of the most popular hospital, Makati Medical Center, where our two younger children were born. I founded and led two nonprofit organizations, the Philippine Association of Childbirth Education and the Nursing Mothers Association of the Philippines, to train Filipina women to carry on my legacy. I wrote and published *A Lamaze Guide for the Philippines*, which was originally published in 1981, went to three editions, and was used in childbirth education classes for years. I also attended dozens of births, including those of several Philippine celebrities, notably Irene Marcos, second daughter of the then president, and — at the other end of the political spectrum — Julie Sison, the wife of the founder of the Communist Party of the Philippines, who delivered in prison at Fort Bonifacio, the national headquarters of the Philippine Army. It was the first and only time, thank goodness, that I've attended a delivery surrounded by machine gun-toting soldiers. I had been asked to attend because Julie and her husband, Jose Maria (Joma) Sison, wanted an impartial witness to ensure truth serum drugs were not administered. Their comrades were still out in the countryside engaged in guerilla warfare, and they didn't want Julie to inadvertently reveal their whereabouts.

I became increasingly interested in maternal and child health, so much so that as soon as I finished my M.A. in Asian studies, I registered to get another master's degree at the University of the Philippines, this time in public health. I loved my classes that focused specifically on maternal and child health but got bogged down in the classes on biostatistics, evaluation, administration, and epidemiology. I was also having second thoughts about the need for a second master's degree. I ended up switching to a doctorate program, not in public health but in political science so I could continue my research on the Chinese Communist Party. These courses were even more interesting than those I had taken for my master's degree; they had titles like "Agrarian Unrest and Peasant Movements in Asia," "Nationalism and National Development," and "Seminar in the Foreign Policy of the Major Powers." I finished all the credits required for the degree, but I was unable to finish my dissertation. The chair of my dissertation committee, Francisco (Dodong) Nemenzo Jr., was in self-imposed exile in Australia to avoid imprisonment as a political dissident. Also, George was working on his Ph.D. dissertation in organizational development, and I figured we needed one of us not to have his or her head in the clouds! Most importantly, I decided I wanted to devote my life to writing, not academia, and I didn't need a Ph.D. to do the kind of journalistic writing I was doing.

Me, Manila (undated)

I had started freelancing in 1975 for several national magazines and newspapers in the Philippines, including *Who* magazine (nothing to do with WHO) and *ExpressWeek*. While I excelled at academic writing and have many published articles to prove it, I found feature writing more creative and fulfilling. I wrote on every topic that struck my fancy, from women's rights to health issues and from culture to politics. However, I steered away from Philippine politics so as not to jeopardize our visas. It was hard in those days. I couldn't do research or fact check on the internet. My sources were old newspaper clippings, encyclopedias for background information, and interviews — lots and lots of interviews. In 1984, I enrolled in the Asian Institute of Journalism, a graduate school in media studies, to take courses I thought might help me in my craft. I completed three trimesters, taking six courses in development journalism and communication theories. The most helpful one was photojournalism, since I was often required to submit my own photographs to accompany the articles I wrote. I published more than 100 articles in the 10 years between 1975 and 1985. I am proud of both the quantity and quality of my writing during that decade, especially given the difficulty of doing research and my many other obligations. Ironically, my classes in maternal and child health and those in journalism — and the portfolio of my writing samples — served me better in my subsequent careers in Switzerland and the U.S. than my master's and unfinished Ph.D.

Part 3: Raising Children in a Foreign Land

The Philippines was a great place to study: its educational institutions were, for the most part, accredited in the U.S.; the quality of its teachers was topnotch; and the tuition and fees were inexpensive, at least for an expat like myself. It was also a great place to raise children. As mentioned earlier, Filipinos are family oriented. Traditionally, they had large families and lived together in multigenerational dwellings. This has changed somewhat in modern times, but when we were living there, children were cherished and could do no wrong. We could take our children to restaurants without fearing dirty looks from other customers or the staff. On the contrary, when one of our children started to fuss or fidget, he or she was swooped up by a waitress and distracted with a toy or something to eat. What a contrast when we moved to Switzerland where people preferred dogs in restaurants to children! With live-in domestic help, our children were nurtured and coddled, oftentimes more than I would have liked.

For a few years, it seemed our firstborn son Greg would be an only child. He had been such a difficult newborn and infant, suffering from what is typically three-month colic for way more than a year. Greg was exclusively breastfed from birth, so it wasn't a reaction to formula, a common cause of colic in bottle-fed babies, and I was careful with what I ate. He cried constantly, from hunger before he ate and from pain afterward, arching his back and flailing his skinny arms and legs. I felt so helpless that I often cried with him as I carried him around, rubbing his small back. My memories of him in his first year were of his little hands clenched into fists and his knees pulled up to his chest, trying to soothe his stomach aches. He almost never slept. It didn't help that we traveled one and a half times around the world in his first nine months. He never adapted to any one time zone.

Greg's first pediatrician gave me phenobarbital to calm him down, but even one drop knocked him out in an abrupt and scary way. I couldn't bear to give it to him. In retrospect, had we been living in the States, with one consistent pediatrician, we might have come up with a better solution. I had little more to go on than a dogeared copy of Dr. Benjamin Spock's *Baby and Child Care* (at one time, the second-best-selling book of all time, after the Bible). The lack of sleep and constant feedings took their toll: by the time Greg was six months old, I was down to 95 pounds, with very dark circles under my eyes, barely able to put one foot in front of the other. It would be months after we arrived in Manila that Greg began to settle down and sleep for more than an hour at a time. As much as I loved Greg and loved being a mother, I couldn't imagine going through that ordeal again.

Greg, with one of his many pets, circa 1972

In the midst of this sleep-deprived and stressful period, I got word that my mother wasn't doing well. (Communications were difficult between Chevy Chase and Manila. Phone calls were expensive, reception was spotty, and there is a 12-hour time difference. We relied primarily on airmail letters.) Against all odds, my mother had survived long enough to welcome Greg into the world and had held him tight when we celebrated Christmas together that year (1971). I had visited her in the hospital and at home after her many surgeries, chemotherapy, and other treatments before we left for Switzerland in early 1972 and again midyear before I left for the Philippines. However, I hadn't seen her in months, during which time her condition had deteriorated. She refused to undergo further treatment — at this point, it seemed worse than the disease. I wanted very much to fly back to Chevy Chase to see her, but I didn't want to travel without Greg, who had just turned a year old, or travel with him given all his sleep and time-adjustment issues. I was heartbroken not to see my mother before she died on February 15, 1973, and not to be able to attend her memorial service the following week. I never got closure; its absence would haunt me for years to come.

The difficult memories of Greg's first year began to fade as he grew into an inquisitive and engaging toddler. Once he was in preschool and I got to know the families of his classmates, I began to see that Greg might benefit from having a sibling or two. Both George and I had wanted more than one child; he had one sibling, I had two. We decided to try again, knowing if we had another colicky infant, we could hire women to take care of him or her while we got some sleep. As soon as I got pregnant, I began recruiting midwifes (glorified nursemaids); I wanted to hire three to work eight-hour shifts around the clock. Like my first pregnancy, my second was easy, with not a bit of morning sickness. I felt balanced and energized, not missing a class at UP while I finished up the coursework for my master's degree. The pendulum had swung when it came to medical advice about weight gain during pregnancy: with my first, I was allowed to gain only 18 pounds; this time, I was told there was no limit. I ended up gaining 36 pounds, twice as much as my first pregnancy, which showed on me and eventually on my Buddha-like newborn whose neck was barely visible between the roundness of his body and his head!

That Chris survived during the months I was carrying him is nothing short of a miracle. I almost lost him twice, once falling off a jumping horse (after which I stopped riding) and once from the sting of a stonefish I inadvertently stepped on in low tide; its venom traveled up my leg and stopped just short of my uterus. The intense throbbing pain from the stonefish sting was almost as excruciating as the birth itself. As a Lamaze instructor, I knew enough about labor to spend most of it at home when I began to feel the signs on September 1, 1975. George took me to the hospital when the contractions were fairly close together and stayed with me the entire time, reminding me to breathe and focus (he hadn't taken a refresher Lamaze course but somehow remembered what to do). My obstetrician was on the tennis court. He rushed into the labor room in his tennis clothes and shoes just in time to catch Chris as he slid out. At first, there was not a sound in the room. I thought my baby was stillborn, and I sat up to look past my draped legs. Chris was just lying quietly on the scale as if trying to figure out how it was calibrated. It was weeks before I heard him cry; mostly he just made small sounds, like he was trying to clear his throat, when he needed to nurse or a diaper change. He must have instinctively known he had to make up for his older brother! In the end, I never needed to hire anyone to help take care of our infant. Chris was just over six months old when I carried him on my hip as I strode up to the stage in my black cap and gown to receive my master's diploma on March 28, 1976.

If we hesitated having a second child, we waited even longer to decide to have a third. We thought it would be nice to have a daughter, but we knew there were no guarantees that we wouldn't have a third son. (That would have been fine with my father-in-law, Leon. My husband was the only son of an only son of an only son. Leon was delighted to already have two grandsons to carry on the Dorros name.) We vacillated, making a list of pros and cons. Although the con column was much longer, the pro side was weighted in favor of wanting a larger family. I have never felt better in my life than when I was pregnant for the third time: I was happy and energized with perfectly balanced hormones. I sailed through the nine months. Right before my due date, George drove me — in the middle of a horrendous typhoon — to the hospital, where my obstetrician had an office. The streets were flooded, and we weren't sure if we would make it to our scheduled appointment. We eventually did and were told that the birth could come any time.

Since we knew it would be one of our last days of peace and quiet, we stopped for a drink at the Intercontinental Hotel near the hospital. As I walked in the door to the lobby of the hotel, my water broke. There was water everywhere, but fortunately people were closing umbrellas and shaking off raincoats and didn't seem to notice. We called the doctor from a pay phone and headed back to the hospital. George and my obstetrician, Conrad ("Clipper") Lorenzo, sat and shot the breeze while I labored. I kept having to remind them I was there! Dr. Lorenzo had agreed to everything we wanted, including the Leboyer method (*Birth Without Violence*) — dimmed lights, soft music, and a warm bath for our newborn right in the delivery room. Our daughter was born peacefully around 8:00 in the evening on July 25, 1980. We named her Sybilla Maria, after me and her paternal grandmother, but it quickly morphed to Samantha and then later to Sam. Our family was now complete with our three children spread over nine years (four years between Greg and Chris and five years between Chris and Sam). I wasn't one of those little girls who dreamt endlessly about motherhood, but I did feel completely fulfilled in my role as a mother. As a newlywed, I had often thought we should have two or four children (I like even numbers!), but three turned out to be perfect.

Dorros family, Manila (undated)

In the absence of biological relatives living close by, we created a network of friends who stood in for them. In the early years, my friend Edith Derting and her husband, John, served as surrogate grandparents for Greg. We frequently met on Saturday mornings to make pork sausage to freeze for later breakfasts, or we gathered to share meals together, especially on American holidays, like Thanksgiving. In subsequent years, many of our friends — Maureen and Van Atkins, Joan and Peter Carl, Susie and Ron Reilly — worked for multinational banks. They became our children's aunts and uncles, often called "Tita" (Aunt) and "Tito" (Uncle) in the Filipino tradition. In some cases, like the Atkins, their children were like cousins to ours. So close were the families that the Atkins left their youngest child, Brenna, with us when they went on home leave one year. As expatriates often relocated or returned to their home countries, we began to befriend more Filipinos and mixed-race couples, where the wife was American and the husband Filipino, like Gail and Tony Rivera and Mary Ellen and Tony de Jesus. When Sam was young, many of my friends were the mothers of her friends, like Sheila West. I also had two special platonic male friends, Jim Stent and John Boyd. Jim was a Sinophile who spoke flawless Mandarin and John was active in our parish. Both were bachelors who seemed to enjoy being included, at different times, in our dinner parties or family outings.

But the people with whom we spent the most time, especially during the later years, were members of the Chanco family. Buena Chanco was initially a professional contact of George's while he was working on his Ph.D. They quickly became close friends, and we ended up spending way too much time at their house — on weekends and to celebrate almost every holiday, including Easter, Christmas, and New Year's Eve. Why they never came to our house remains a mystery. At the time, the Chancos had three children (they later had one more), similar in ages to ours, but with little else in common; they went to different schools and had their own friends and interests. I had zero in common with Buena's husband, Poyo, and the two of us often sat in an uncomfortable silence while Buena and George chattered animatedly about professional issues and their mutual friends. Buena was attractive and always stylishly dressed, with her hair perfectly coiffed and her makeup flawless, even in the sweltering heat. I became extremely jealous of her as George's eyes would follow her as she sashayed across the room in her high-heeled shoes. Our kids and I began to dread our visits to the Chanco home, but George insisted we spend time there. He also insisted, over my very fervent objections, that Buena should be Sam's godmother. It was clear that he was smitten with Buena and she with him.

George also insisted that the kids, especially Greg, who was not attending a Catholic school, receive religious instruction at San Antonio Parish, a parish that catered to English-speaking expatriates. I disagreed: I felt it was hypocritical to make the kids get religious instruction and attend mass, if we — their parents — were not also doing so. George and I had left the Catholic Church in the early 1970s, along with many other rebellious youths, over the injustices in the church and various social issues, like birth control. George was not ready to go back, but I refused to relent on this issue, "Either we all go to church as a family, or no one goes." This was one of our knock-down, drag-out fights I wasn't prepared to lose — and I didn't. It marked the beginning of our slow reentry into the Catholic Church. San Antonio's parish priest, Father Hugh Zurat, an American Franciscan who spent nearly 30 years serving in the Philippines, warmly welcomed us and allowed us to reintegrate at our own pace. It wasn't long before we were actively involved in various ministries, including teaching catechism and leading retreats. I was confirmed by Father Hugh, a sacrament I had somehow missed when I converted to Catholicism in college. Greg and Chris became altar servers (girls were not allowed to at that time), and all three kids performed in the church's Christmas and Easter pageants. They probably don't remember a time when we didn't go to church as a family. Father Hugh baptized Sam when she was a few months old, with Buena as her godmother.

Part 4: Solo and Family Adventures

When Sam was just six weeks old, I was recruited to a new job with Organization Resources Counselors (ORC), a New York-based management consulting firm that provided services, including cost-of-living comparisons, to U.S. corporations. I had previously worked for ORC for about five years as a pricing agent, collecting the data that would be used in the Manila cost-of-living computations. Now they wanted me to manage the pricing agents in 15 locations in a region that spanned from Pakistan to Guam and from Korea to New Zealand. I initially turned down the offer, but ORC was persistent. They finally agreed to all my demands, including that Sam could travel with me on business trips until she was a year old and ostensibly weaned. Sam and I took off almost immediately to Australia, stopping in Sydney to meet the pricing agent there and then traveling on to Canberra to meet with my predecessor and collect his files. It was the first of many trips we took together, including ones to Okinawa and Hong Kong. Over the next five years, as Sam got older, I left her at home as I traveled to places like Bangladesh, Pakistan, Indonesia, Brunei, Borneo, Korea, and Japan. I occasionally took one of the boys with me, Greg to Taiwan and Chris to Thailand, or had them meet me somewhere like Hong Kong. I loved the traveling and the chance to sit quietly on a plane or in a hotel room and read a book — a real luxury given my busy life in Manila.

I also traveled frequently to China with the Association of Philippine-China Understanding (APCU), a people-to-people friendship organization that paved the way for diplomatic relations between the two countries. As a China scholar, I was on the board of APCU and was editor-in-chief of its newsletter, *The China Reader*. I was part of the first APCU delegation to China in 1978, just two years after the death of Mao and the end of the Cultural Revolution. At that time, there were no direct flights between Manila and Beijing. We had to fly into Hong Kong (still under British rule) and take the train to the Chinese border. There, we walked across the border, dragging our suitcases, into Shenzhen — then still a sleepy fishing village — and boarded another train to Guangzhou (Canton). Now, you can take a high-speed train directly from Hong Kong to Guangzhou, but in those days, the gauge of the tracks was different. Once in China, we saw virtually no cars on the road, even in the large cities like Beijing and Shanghai, only bicycles and more bicycles. Everyone — men, women, and children —wore baggy blue pants and jackets. The country was poor and disadvantaged after 10 years of civil strife. Over the years, I traveled extensively around China, witnessing firsthand the remarkable changes that took place after the country was opened to trade and tourism.

We traveled as a family within the Philippines and had our share of adventures. We camped on one of the uninhabited Hundred Islands in the Lingayen Gulf in the northern Philippines. We spent many Holy Weeks on the island of Marinduque in the South, where each year during the seven-day Moriones Festival, local residents dress up in elaborate costumes and helmets reminiscent of biblical times and reenact Jesus's crucifixion. A leading role is given to Longinus, the near-blind soldier who punctures Jesus with his spear and has his sight restored. We tried to shield the kids from the more gruesome reenactments, such as bloody flagellations along the roads on Good Friday and, in some parts of the Philippines, actual crucifixions (the people who volunteer to be crucified in atonement for their sins are taken down from the cross before they die).

We visited the island of Leyte, where George was working on a WHO project with the Ministry of Health, and saw the larger-than-life statue of General Douglas MacArthur wading ashore on one of its beaches in 1944. We had a trip planned to Mindanao, the southern-most part of the Philippines, in 1975, but there had been a number of kidnappings of foreigners, and we ended up in Bali, Indonesia, instead. Mostly, we just hung out at our beach house in Matabungkay; we shared the house with another family and were able to use it every other weekend and some holidays. The house had no electricity or running water, so it was incredibly basic. But we loved our time there, walking on the beach, barbecuing, snorkeling, and sleeping under the stars on our wraparound porch with built-in benches we covered with kapok mattresses.

At our beach house in Matabungkay (undated)

We had very few visitors while we lived in Manila. George's parents came once to spend Christmas with us, my father came after my mother died in 1973, his sister — my aunt Dorothy — visited briefly when she was on an Asian tour, and a few friends passed through on business or on vacation. The only exception was my cousin Robert White, who had worked for years in the Middle East and was then living in Hong Kong. He flew in regularly for holidays and family occasions and could be counted on to bring us whatever treats we were craving. He kept us well stocked with French wines and Swiss chocolates.

Part 5: Turbulent Departure

Toward the end of our 14-year stay in the Philippines, the political situation began to disintegrate, starting on August 21, 1983, with the assassination of Benigno (Ninoy) Aquino Jr., a former Philippine senator, on the tarmac of Manila International Airport as he returned from self-exile in the U.S. Aquino's assassination transformed the opposition to the Marcos regime from a small, isolated movement into a national one. It also brought Aquino's widow, Corazon (Cory) Aquino, into the public spotlight; she ran for president in 1986. In the months running up to this snap election, the streets of Manila were filled with people participating in pro-Marcos or pro-Aquino campaign rallies. Our inventive driver, Dong, had two flags and two T-shirts: when we approached a pro-Marcos rally, he slipped on his red, white, and blue T-shirt and draped the corresponding flag on the outside of our car; likewise, approaching a pro-Aquino rally, it was a yellow T-shirt and yellow flag. In this way, we were able to navigate the streets and get to the stores or the kids' extracurricular activities unscathed. (Many of the rallies turned violent, and cars deemed to be the opposition were attacked.)

Marcos was officially declared the winner of the election, but widespread allegations of fraud against him sparked the People Power Revolution. By the time of the 1986 election and subsequent revolution, I was alone in Manila with our two younger children (Greg was in boarding school in Hawaii). George had been reassigned to WHO headquarters in Geneva and had gone ahead, departing Manila at the beginning of January. We decided I should stay on in Manila so Chris could finish his school year. He was in fourth grade, and school was due to end in March (summer was April and May in the Filipino academic calendar). I was used to being on my own, but these were not ordinary times. We lived not far from the military base from which tanks and helicopters were sent to disperse the protesters. The helicopters hovered close enough to the house to blow around the papers on my desk. I was scared out of my wits and had no one to turn to for support, but I kept on a brave face for the sake of the children. I tried to pretend that everything was just fine, even though it was clear, even to them, it was not. They couldn't go to school (our reason for staying) or their extracurricular activities, as the entire city was locked down.

It was hard for me to figure out what was happening since the military had taken over all the TV and radio stations. The only news I was occasionally able to get was from the BBC on my little transistor radio. And it was the first time in my 14 years in the Philippines that the mood had turned decidedly anti-American: the protesters yelled chants like "Down with the Reagan-Marcos dictatorship." (President Reagan had moved slowly in withdrawing his support for Marcos, and even when he did, he granted the entire Marcos family asylum in Hawaii.) I hunkered down at home, as did most of my friends, and in the midst of all the political upheaval, I never got to say goodbye to them before I left. The People Power Revolution resulted in President Marcos conceding the presidency to Cory Aquino and leaving the country with his family on February 25, 1986. Coincidently, three weeks later, the kids and I followed them to Honolulu, where we stayed for a week to catch our breath following our tumultuous departure from Manila. Then we made our way across the U.S., visiting family and friends, before moving on to Switzerland. Our 14-year stay in the Philippines had been fundamentally peaceful but bookended at the beginning and the end by political upheaval.

Back to the Future

Geneva (April 1986 – July 1995)

I turned 40 years old as my flight landed at Geneva's Cointrin Airport in the early morning hours of April 19, 1986. Back when I was making my travel arrangements, I hadn't really planned it, but it turned out to be a perfect way to mark that milestone. Spring was in full bloom in Switzerland, and the weather was mild. George had met Sam and me and had driven us straight to a little café with an outdoor patio along Lake Geneva. It was an unusually clear day, and we could see across to the other side of the lake to one of the city's most famous landmarks, the Jet d'Eau, a fountain that spouts water more than 400 feet into the air. More surprisingly, the magnificent Mont Blanc was visible. Often the iconic mountain is shrouded in clouds, but on this day, its snow-capped peak looked like it had been painted on the blue sky. After our continental breakfast, we walked across the street to get a closer look at the lake and the graceful white swans gliding on its surface. I was overwhelmed by the beauty of the surroundings, especially the flowers; they were everywhere in the garden beds that lined this pristine city's lakeshore sidewalk. After 14 years of living in a developing country's dirty, polluted metropolis, the contrast couldn't have been starker. I kept repeating over and over to myself and George, "I think I've died and gone to Heaven."

This was my second move to Geneva. My first had been more than 20 years earlier when I studied there during my junior year abroad from college. As we walked around the streets (my trick for adjusting to jet lag), I was astonished at how little had changed in two decades. Yes, a McDonald's had opened on the rue de Mont-Blanc, just a couple of doors down from the Café de Paris, which had been my favorite restaurant when I lived there as a student. (When I finally went back to the Café de Paris, I found the menu hadn't changed; in fact, it hadn't changed since 1930 when the restaurant first opened. They still served only one option: salad and an entrecôte with French fries.) The hotels and stores were unchanged. Even the people looked the same, although the younger ones now wore jeans, T-shirts, and athletic shoes. Geneva had always had a large number of foreigners because of the international organizations (WHO, ILO, IMO, WMO, UNHCR, etc.) but now had noticeably more, including large entourages of Arabs going in and out of the high-end stores, like Louis Vuitton. Nonetheless, the city seemed familiar to me, and I was delighted to be back for Round 2.

George had been renting a small one-bedroom apartment on a month-to-month basis since he arrived in January, with the understanding I would start house hunting as soon as I arrived. For the time being, there were only the three of us — George, five-year-old Sam, and me — so the quarters, while cramped, were sufficient for a short-term stay. Greg was finishing up ninth grade in boarding school on the Big Island of Hawaii, and we left Chris with his grandparents in Tucson for an extended visit. They would travel together to Switzerland in late June, and all three kids would attend summer camps that included instruction in French. The boys had been accepted at the International School of Geneva (La Châtaigneraie campus on the right bank of Lake Geneva, 20 minutes outside the city) for the coming fall, but Sam had not; there was a year-long waiting list for first grade. She was to attend Collège du

Léman, a Swiss day and boarding school that catered to the children of the world's elites. In the long run, it was a good choice of school for her, but it wasn't convenient having the kids in two schools with different scholastic calendars. I also knew it was going to be tough with Sam not having any friends in Geneva until camp started. So, we went straight to Collège du Léman, where I begged the principal and the kindergarten teacher to admit her for the last six weeks of the current school year. It ran against their policies, and the kindergarten class was at capacity, but they finally relented. It was a godsend for me to have a few hours a day to find a place to live and for Sam to be able to begin her adjustment to a foreign country. (At that time, she considered herself a Filipina since she was born in Manila.)

Exactly one week after Sam and I arrived, on April 26, the nuclear accident at Chernobyl took place. While Chernobyl is more than 1,500 miles from Geneva, we nonetheless felt the effects of what is still considered the worst nuclear disaster in history. Four days after the explosion, the radioactive cloud reached Switzerland. We were told to avoid fresh milk and bought extended shelf-life Tetra Paks of milk that had been processed prior to the accident. Rumors abounded about the fish, especially from the worst hit area around Lake Lugano, and fresh vegetables. If radioactivity was found in fresh milk, it was probably also in the cows and their meat, but I don't remember being warned about eating beef. In 2006, 20 years after Chernobyl, Switzerland was still affected by higher-than-normal rates of radioactivity, with an estimated 200 deaths from cancer a direct result. In hindsight, we should have probably taken more precautions than we did. At the time, we were laser-focused on getting settled in as quickly as humanely possible.

I spoke fluent French. In fact, I had taught French at the Alliance Française in Manila for several years. However, my vocabulary was rusty, and I had never needed to know terms related to the rental market, like security deposit and lease termination. Moreover, I had no idea about rents in Geneva, and it was only by scouring the want ads in the newspapers (before the days of internet searching) that I figured out where we could afford to live and what we could get for 30% of George's salary (less wasn't feasible given the high cost of living in Geneva). I saw dozens of places, tootling around in our brand-new Volvo station wagon and armed only with a printed map. I finally found a house that met our needs: it was at the end of a cul-de-sac in Commugny, halfway between the train station in Coppet (to get in and out of Geneva) and the boys' school in La Châtaigneraie. It had three bedrooms and a family room that could serve as a fourth and sat perched on a little hill overlooking farmlands with sheep and the lake in the distance. Coincidently, it was owned by an administrator at Collège du Léman, which gave us a slight edge over the other applicants. George signed the lease, and we impatiently waited for our shipment of furniture and household items to arrive via slow boat from Manila.

On the first day I dropped off Sam at kindergarten at Collège du Léman, I met Mike O'Neil, who was also dropping off his daughter, Kateri. Mike introduced himself and told me I should meet his wife, Maryvelma (MV), who was working on her doctoral dissertation. I met MV later that week, and we became lifelong friends. Sam and Kateri, along with a slew of their classmates, remained friends from kindergarten until Sam left at the end of ninth grade and beyond. Sam and Kateri were especially close. Sam went on vacations with the O'Neils, and Kateri came on vacations with us. Indeed, many of our friends were the parents of our kids' friends. By and large, most were expatriates living in Switzerland. The only Swiss friends I made were the spouses of foreigners, like Pierre Gavillet, the husband of my good friend Marianne, who is Swedish. Most Swiss tended not to reach out to foreigners; unlike Filipinos, they are not hospitable by nature and assume the expats will stay in their country only temporarily.

The summer went by quickly, and by the fall of 1986, we were settled in to our new life in Switzerland. The boys rode their bikes (later mopeds) to school; Sam took the bus in the morning, and I picked her up after school to take her to her extracurricular activities, which included gymnastics across the border in France. I bought a secondhand Peugeot to get around, especially for frequent, almost daily, grocery shopping, since the refrigerator was so small and our growing boys' appetites were so big. Two or more times a week, George made an early morning run to the bakery in the next town to get fresh-out-of-the-oven croissants, *pain au chocolat*, baguettes, and loaves of multigrain bread for sandwiches. He often went to the Saturday market in France to buy cold cuts, cheeses, olives, and wine — it became something of a ritual for him, stopping for a coffee and later lunch, as he haggled with the mostly North African merchants. I, on the other hand, spent my Saturdays at the supermarket buying more practical items, like paper products and nonperishables. Yes, a big part of our time was spent shopping, cooking, and cleaning — without the support of the kind of domestic help we had in the Philippines. Before we moved to Geneva, one of my biggest worries was that I would be housebound doing most of the chores. Except for a Filipina who came in once a week to do the heavy cleaning, I did indeed take on the lion's share of the housework, made all the more tedious by the inefficient European appliances. For example, the washing machine was so small, it could only handle one king-size sheet at a time.

It didn't take long to figure out that I needed to get out of the house and find a job. Few spouses, still mostly wives, of the international civil servants were able to work. Swiss labor laws were strict, working permits hard to come by, and the international organizations frowned on hiring "trailing spouses." I managed to circumvent these restrictions by getting hired at Webster University in Geneva, the Swiss campus of the St. Louis-based Webster University. For five years (1987–1992), I worked as the manager of its 3,000-volume bookstore, with annual sales of more than $150,000. I was able to hire one student assistant to help me with sales and lugging boxes around during the busy hours at the beginning of each term, but mostly I was on my own to do all the ordering, organizing, inventorying, accounting, and consulting with instructors on their textbooks. It was a thankless job, and I was delighted when I was invited to teach and could give it up. I then became a lecturer in the International Relations Department for three years (1992–1994), teaching one course per eight-week term. I taught various courses, including Modern Chinese History (from the Opium Wars to the then present) and Comparative Politics and Economics: China and Vietnam. I was also the editor of the university's quarterly magazine, *The Web.* I researched and wrote articles and edited the content submitted by others. During part of the time when I was working at Webster, Greg was a student there; it gave me an instant entrée into happenings on campus and student life.

As I was teaching only part-time at Webster, I also did freelance writing and editing for various international organizations. My first assignment was with the United Nations' Department of Humanitarian Affairs (1992–1993), working with senior staff in gathering information on humanitarian crises and relief activities primarily in Africa and the former Yugoslavia. At the World Health Organization, where I worked for a couple of years (1993–1995), I used my background in maternal and child health to write and edit brochures and manuals on best practices in childbirth and breastfeeding, often dealing with sensitive issues like HIV transmission to newborns from their mothers and complications from abortions. (Because George was on staff at WHO, I couldn't be hired full-time, but I signed two 11-month contracts.)

During this time, I edited five issues of *FOCUS*, the newsletter of a nonprofit organization called International Career Services, geared primarily to expatriate women. I was hired by the International Federation of Red Cross and Red Crescent Societies (IFRC) to replace a woman on maternity leave (1994–1995). There, I had the privilege of working with Kathy Ramsperger, the editor of the IFRC magazine; she and I had a wonderful working relationship and have kept in touch ever since — more than a quarter century later. I wrote two bylined articles published in the magazine: "Brave Beginnings," about tailoring humanitarian assistance to the needs of women, and

"Raising Funds," on how national Red Cross societies are finding creative ways to generate resources. I edited several manuals for trainers on topics such as first aid and drafted a history of the IFRC for its 75th anniversary celebration in 1994. I was hired separately to work on three issues of *Transfusion International*, a newsletter of the IFRC devoted to all things related to blood transfusions. In early 1994, I finished the first draft of "Women Workers: An Annotated Bibliography" for the International Labour Office. These contracts were relatively well paid, and we used this extra income to finance our vacations and other luxuries; George's salary and cost-of-living allowance covered our basic living expenses and necessities.

Because we lived *on* the beaten path in Europe, we had lots of visitors over the years. George's parents came several times. On one occasion, we traveled together to Europe's highest railroad station, an underground station at Jungfraujoch, stayed in Lucerne with its preserved medieval architecture and pristine lake, and ate our way through various cantons (similar to states in the U.S.). George's sister, Miriam, also visited with her then husband, Michael. My two sisters came separately, Eleanor on her way to a conference in France and Kathy doing a solo sightseeing trip to Germany. My high school roommate Ann Miller Riggan and her husband, John, came to Geneva, and then we traveled together to Italy, visiting nostalgic places from our boarding school days. Rome was extra special, since George, Ann, and I had all been there together nearly three decades earlier. My college roommate Christiane Corbat Westlake came several times with her husband, Bob, and their two daughters; they were regular visitors since Christiane had many relatives still living in Geneva (her grandmother had since passed away).

My father came once to visit us in Geneva. By then, he was in his 80s and was living in a retirement community in Washington, D.C. He had dementia but still functioned well enough to travel on his own (unbeknownst to him as an "unaccompanied senior" for his plane change in Paris). One of the last uncompleted items on his lifetime bucket list was to go to the opera in Vienna, and I was determined to make it happen. I booked us a week-long trip to Vienna and purchased opera tickets for all but one evening. Unlike the rest of my family of origin, I am not an opera buff, so I picked out the lightest operas I could find, like *The Marriage of Figaro*, *The Barber of Seville*, and *La Bohème*. (Vienna has three major opera houses plus several minor ones.) My father never commented on my selection; he either didn't notice or didn't care. He was just ecstatic to be at the opera in Vienna. On our non-opera evening, we went to a musical, Andrew Lloyd Webber's *Cats* in German.

During the day, we crammed in a busy schedule of sightseeing — churches, museums, and a behind-the-scenes tour of the Vienna State Opera house, plus a stop at Demel for a slice of Vienna's most famous chocolate cake, the Sachertorte. There was no way, as a former equestrian, I was going to visit Vienna without seeing the famous Lipizzaner stallions. I had seen these dancing horses in films, but it was thrilling to see them prancing around right in front of us (I had snagged us front row seats). One day, we went to a concert by the Vienna Boys' Choir, consisting of about 100 boys between the ages of 9 and 14 in their trademark sailor-suit uniforms. I had seen them once before in the States, but it was special to hear their angelic voices reverberate in the Imperial Chapel of the Hofburg Palace. On our last full day, we took a bus tour of the Austrian countryside, through charming villages and scenic landscapes of the Wachau Valley. We ate what was billed as an authentic Austrian lunch at a local wine tavern and took a Danube River cruise. Everywhere we went, my father took copious notes in a small notebook he kept in the breast pocket of his jacket. He wanted to savor every moment. We reviewed what we did several times a day so he might be able to remember some of the details of the trip once he returned to the States.

We often took our out-of-town visitors to an authentic fondue luncheon in the picturesque town of Gruyères, a medieval town in the Fribourg canton known for its production of the cheese of the same name. In fact, we went so often the waitresses in the restaurant we frequented began to recognize us. We regularly went to Taizé, an ecumenical Christian monastery in Burgundy, France. We would attend a Sunday morning service at the monastery and then head into the town of Mâcon for a decadent French midday meal before driving the 100 miles back to Geneva, stopping first to pick up some local Burgundy wines for the onslaught of visitors.

We also went to Taizé with members of our English-speaking parish, John XXIII, and to help chaperone the teenagers during their Confirmation retreat there. I volunteered on a regular basis at John XXIII, spearheading its welcome committee and serving as the adult education coordinator. This meant endless meetings, including a monthly parish council meeting, and eventually training to become a small group leader for our parish renewal program and a presenter with George for Marriage Encounter weekends. Both boys went through the parish's two-year Confirmation program, and Sam attended religious education classes. All in all, we spent an extreme amount of time at John XXIII, but it helped solidify my Catholic faith that had faltered in the States in the early 1970s and had been rekindled in the Philippines in the early 1980s. My parish work also led to a lifelong friendship with our pastor, Father Peter Henry. Father Peter joined our family every February when we spent a week skiing in Verbier and was a regular guest at meals at our house and at birthday and anniversary celebrations in restaurants, almost always in neighboring France — Divonne-les-Bains, Thonon, or Annecy. In later years and before he died in June 2021, Father Peter often reminisced about these memorable times with our family.

Fr. Peter with Sam after her First Communion at John XXIII

My life in Geneva was a study in contrasts — the mundane, day-to-day activities carried out in an often cold, damp, overcast, and xenophobic city, punctuated by moments of pure bliss, hiking or skiing in the Alps or the Jura, above the clouds in abundant sunshine and crystal-clear air. I often thought I would have gone crazy if it had not been for the chance to escape to the incomparable beauty of nature in Switzerland and neighboring France. My job at Webster University was part-time, so I could juggle my hours to get a weekday off to head to the mountains by myself or with a friend. Or George and I would abandon our weekend chores and errands and take off for a day of hiking or skiing, with or without the kids. It was such a luxury to live in a country where our teenage sons could go off with their friends on a train to the city center or go skiing by themselves without having to worry about them being kidnapped! Sam had dozens of friends, and we traded off sleepovers with their families. (Sam was well-traveled; she accompanied friends all over Europe and took an educational cruise around the Mediterranean with her school.) Traveling in Europe was expensive for a family of five, so we usually limited ourselves to two vacations a year: our ski trip in February and a trip to the beaches of Southern France in the summer. Once, at the end of 1992, we all went on the spur of the moment to Corsica, the fourth-largest island in the Mediterranean, to celebrate New Year's, taking the overnight 12-hour car ferry from Marseilles, but that was the exception, not the rule. There was no way we could keep up with the Swiss, many of whom used their six weeks of vacation per year to travel worldwide!

I took one trip on my own. Because I was teaching Chinese Studies at Webster University, I was asked to co-lead its first-ever business study tour to China in October 1992. Business majors could take the two-week tour for credit, provided they fulfilled the requirements, including a small group project to be completed in China and a final paper shortly after their return. Webster figured it would be more lucrative to have a larger group and opened it to the public. The final tally was 20 students and 20 mostly Swiss tourists, an unwieldly size to manage, especially in a foreign country where no one, except me, spoke the language, in this case Mandarin. We flew to Beijing on Finnish Airlines with a one-night, two-day stopover to sightsee in Helsinki. Once in China, for our students, we visited some of the major industrial cities in the country, including Shanghai, Shenzhen, Guangzhou, and as we exited the country, Hong Kong, five years before it was transferred back to China. And for our tourists: Nanjing (China's ancient capital), Xian (to see the famous Terracotta Warriors), Chengdu (the home of China's giant pandas), and Chongqing, where we boarded the boat for our Yangtze River cruise.

I have never heard so much grumbling and complaining in my life! The students didn't like the food and went out for Western dinners every night, even though they had prepaid a Chinese meal in the hotel restaurant. The tourists got bored going to factories, and the students were uninterested in the historical sites, except for the Great Wall. We eventually split up the two groups and worked out a different itinerary for each, which was complicated at times when we had hired only a single bus in each city. Things had improved immensely until my co-leader's wife fell on the train going to Xian; she badly injured her face on the shards of a ceramic plate she was carrying from the dining car. She chose to be airlifted to Hong Kong for plastic surgery rather than having it done in Xian. My co-leader accompanied her, and I was left to manage the entire group of 40 by myself. Fortunately, we were near the end of our trip, and we met up again in Hong Kong with the co-leader and his wife before flying back to Geneva. Any thought I had harbored about becoming a professional tour guide went out the window after this trip!

George and I also tried to squeeze in a weekend getaway at least once a year, usually around his birthday in November. Unlike me, George loved surprises, so I would dream up elaborate plans to get him to some secret destination without him knowing where he was going. I would tell him what clothes he needed to pack and that was it. He wouldn't know where we would be staying or what mode of transportation we would be taking. One time, we took the train to Saas-Fee, a car-free resort village in the Swiss Alps, and rode in a horse-drawn sleigh to the hotel. Another time, we drove to a French resort on the other side of Lake Geneva. I had arranged a day of white-water rafting, canyoneering, and rappelling on the Dranse River, activities I found exhilarating, but he hated. That was my only failed venture.

My most elaborate ruse involved getting him to London in November 1991. I made him wait to the side while I checked us in at the airport and deliberately took him to the wrong gate. It wasn't until our final boarding call that he knew where we were headed. He had a wonderful time. We met up with an old friend of his for a birthday dinner at the Elephant & Castle Pub (motto: "Get Your Brit On!"); visited Canary Wharf and enjoyed a cruise on the River Thames; went Christmas window-shopping at Harrods (the sidewalks were so congested with holiday shoppers, British police officers — Bobbies — were directing pedestrian traffic); took a short train ride out to Greenwich to see the Royal Observatory (site of the Greenwich meridian line); and attended a theatrical performance of

Les Misérables. George kept shaking his head as if he couldn't believe he was actually in London! To say that we took advantage of living in the heart of Europe would be an understatement. And for the most part, life was good.

It was a gorgeous Saturday in the spring of 1994 when George suggested we go out to dinner that night, just the two of us. Sam would be at a sleepover, and our boys were no longer living at home. What's not to like about a date night when you've been married nearly 26 years? Better yet, George had made reservations at one of my favorite restaurants, a small Indian one in the middle of the Swiss countryside. It might seem strange to crave Indian food in Switzerland, but the restaurant was authentic, and you can only eat so much cheese fondue, raclette, entrecôte, French fries, and rösti in one lifetime! I dressed with care, putting on my pretty pink two-piece suit that epitomized springtime, paired with a flouncy white blouse that wasn't really my style but seemed more feminine than my usual workday ones. As we drove to the restaurant, I recalled my first day in Geneva eight years earlier when all the spring flowers were in bloom. Here, outside the city, the bright yellow rapeseed (canola) flowers were just beginning to bud, but the colorful wildflowers I loved so much when I was hiking covered the meadows to either side of the winding road. Everywhere I looked was postcard perfect.

Once settled at our table in the restaurant, George ordered a small pitcher of red wine for himself and an Indian Kingfisher beer for me. *Who drinks red wine with Indian food?* I asked myself, but then recalled we were in Switzerland, not India. George seemed distracted, but he often did, especially when a lot was going on at the office. He had worked at WHO for more than two decades and had been given more responsibilities with seniority. As I was biting into one of the delicately fried samosas we had ordered to share, George said, "I can't take it anymore." I hadn't a clue what he was talking about. He must have noticed the blank look on my face. "This marriage isn't working for me," he added. "I want out." My brain was having trouble processing the words, but my gut felt sucker punched. One doesn't raise one's voice in a restaurant in Switzerland, so I just sat there, stunned speechless. I only heard bits and pieces of what he said next, words like "trapped," "imprisoned," and "loveless." *How could this be?* I asked myself. I knew our marriage wasn't perfect, but I never in a million years expected it to end over an Indian appetizer. I asked the waiter to box up the rest of our order — chicken curry, spinach vindaloo, red lentil dahl, and naan — and to bring the check. I couldn't get out of there fast enough.

George moved out the next day. He had secretly rented a small apartment not far from the house we had lived in together for the last eight years. I watched mutely as he packed his suitcases and several boxes of possessions that he deemed his. He had sat Sam down earlier to explain what was happening. "Are you divorcing us?" she asked. She seemed to consider her father's leaving as much of an affront as I did. It was hard for me to understand, much less explain to a 13-year-old why this was happening and so suddenly. In hindsight, it was a perfect storm of milestones and events, including George's 50th birthday just months before and a recent near-death experience from a case of cerebral malaria in Guinea Bissau (this can cause cognitive and behavioral changes). It was a full-blown midlife crisis with repercussions far more serious than the purchase of a new red sports car. "I don't want a divorce," he claimed. "Just a separation. I want to live my own life — my life, not ours." He wanted to quit his job (he didn't), and he wanted to leave Switzerland (he didn't). As George continued to chronicle all the things that were missing in his life, I kept hearing the refrain of Peggy Lee's song from the 1960s, "Is That All There Is?" But the lyrics didn't fit. The singer wanted to: "… keep dancing … break out the booze and have a ball …" None of that was going to happen, except perhaps the booze part.

For the next few months, we had to explain to family and friends why we were no longer living together. No one would believe we were separated — we who presented Marriage Encounter weekends and were a model couple in our community. I kept saying, "George is going through a bad patch," and "This is only temporary," and "I'm sure we'll get back together." I was saying this as much to reassure myself as for them. When summer came, Sam and I took off on a round-the-world trip. Every two years, WHO gave us the equivalent of roundtrip business class tickets to Tucson, Arizona, considered our home base. We could go anywhere we liked as long as we spent a minimum of two weeks in Tucson. Sam left before me and flew by herself to Bangladesh to visit a school friend and then on to Hong Kong, where I met her and Chris, who was studying in Beijing. The three of us spent a few fabulous days doing all the touristy stuff, riding the Star Ferry and gorging on Chinese food. We also visited with their former nanny, Terry, who had relocated to work in Hong Kong after we left Manila. Chris flew back to Beijing, and Sam and I went on to Manila so I could reconnect with old friends and Sam could revisit her birthplace. The city had become even more polluted and congested, if that were possible; I felt grateful to no longer be living there. Sam and I stopped in Honolulu, Tucson, and Washington, D.C., as we made our way across the U.S. and eventually back to Geneva. I returned refreshed and revitalized, even more optimistic that George and I would be able to get back together again.

It wasn't meant to be. I consulted a legal officer at WHO about my status. She advised me to stay married and "milk the son of a bitch" (her words, not mine) for all he was worth. If I stayed married, Sam and I could remain on his health insurance and reap all his other benefits, like tuition reimbursement for Sam's private high school and college. If later George wanted a divorce to remarry, he would have to buy me out. It sounded like a good deal, but it didn't take into consideration the fact that my visa to stay in Switzerland was tied to George's and married women in Switzerland were not able to sign a lease, open a bank account, or do anything without her husband's written approval. Swiss women weren't even able to vote until 1971!

I couldn't imagine having to ask George to sign my lease or to be beholden to him on so many levels. What if I did something to anger him and he took away my banking privileges? I researched the residency laws in several states, including Maryland, Massachusetts, and California, to see how long I would have to live there before I could file for a divorce. Most required six months' residency, and I was concerned that, in the meantime, George might file for divorce in Switzerland, and I would be considered at fault for "kidnapping" our daughter (leaving the country with her without his permission). My hands were tied: I had no choice but to file for divorce myself in Switzerland before I moved back to the States, where I hoped to be able to better support Sam and myself. It didn't feel right: George was the one who had left our marriage, but I took the blame for the divorce. Moreover, the divorce agreement was skewed against me as the wife. I would have gotten a much better settlement in the States. As I told my children on so many occasions when they were growing up, "Life is not fair."

Once more, I packed my bags, said my goodbyes, and steeled myself for the next chapter in my life in yet another new place — this time as a divorcée and single mother of a teenage girl. It was indeed an unceremonious end to an otherwise idyllic nine-year sojourn in Switzerland, leading to yet another global relocation — or, in this case, dislocation.

The Long Road Home

Forever (July 1995 – Present)

Part 1: Crash Landing in Braintree

Sam and I returned to the States in July 1995. I hadn't known where to go since America wasn't really my home anymore. I had been away off and on for more than 40 years. The logical choice would have been the Maryland suburbs where I had grown up or somewhere else in the greater metropolitan Washington, D.C., area. However, I had lived in that area as a newlywed and didn't want to go somewhere that had so many memories of a happier time and constant reminders of my failed marriage. I was tempted by California, but it seemed so far away from any family or friends, and I wanted Sam to be able to travel easily to Geneva on her vacations to visit her father.

I settled on Boston, where I had lived for a year when I first graduated from college. It was familiar, and above all, Massachusetts had a good public college education system should George renege on his agreement to pay for Sam's tuition through her bachelor's degree. Over the previous spring break, Sam had gone to Boston to check it out for herself and to choose a high school. A relocated friend from Geneva drove her around, and Sam picked Thayer Preparatory

Academy in Braintree. I had never heard of Braintree before, but it suited me fine once I learned it was on both the subway and commuter rail line into Boston and Cambridge, the two places where I would probably end up working.

I made the decision to move back to the States, and to the Boston area in particular, with my head. It was rational and practical. However, it didn't take my heart — or Sam's — into consideration. We were miserable. We were summarily removed from the country that had been our home for nine years, away from our family and friends, and dropped into a community that seemed totally foreign, despite my earlier time living and vacationing in Massachusetts. I knew less than a handful of people — my cousin Newell and two relocated friends from Geneva. Sam would sit staring out the window for hours. Once when I asked her what was wrong, she gave me a litany of her losses: "I lost my father. I lost my brothers. I lost my school. I lost my friends. I even lost my cat."

Our new rental in Braintree didn't allow pets, and Sam had to leave her beloved cat, Jimmy, in Geneva. Jimmy became emblematic of everything we were leaving behind. Sam and I stood in the vet's office with tears streaming down our faces as we explained to the vet that we had to put Jimmy to sleep since we couldn't take him with us. The vet, an obvious animal lover and an immigrant who had left his own country, empathized with our situation and gave us time and space to grieve. However, he said emphatically, "There is no way I'm going to put down this young and healthy cat. I will find a good home for him." Sam wasn't convinced: she didn't want Jimmy to have to adapt to a new home the way she knew she was going to have to. The vet reassured her, "If I can't find the perfect home for him, I will keep him myself." We stroked Jimmy one last time, kissed the top of his furry little head, and with heavy hearts, walked out of the vet's office.

The isolation and dislocation I felt in Braintree were overwhelming at times. I was particularly devastated by the fact that George's parents, Marie and Leon, whom I had grown to love as my own, blamed me for the divorce. Of course, they were going to take the side of their son, who had always been treated like a prince and who, in their eyes, could do no wrong. During our 27-year marriage, they had treated me like their daughter. In fact, Marie often introduced me as her daughter. Despite the fact that I was a bit too much of a feminist for their liking in the late 1960s, they always supported me in my work and my causes. Leon revered me once I gave birth to our first son to carry on the Dorros name. The fact that I had a second son was icing on the cake. When Chris was born, his grandfather had just had quadruple bypass surgery. I rushed Chris to Tucson so Leon could meet his second grandson and witness Chris's baptism. I considered my bond with Marie and Leon indissoluble, so my rejection was all the more painful. They refused to speak to me after I visited Tucson in 1994 and didn't for nearly 20 years. Throughout that time, I continued to write to them and send them photos of the kids. It wasn't until Leon fell gravely ill that I was invited for a visit. Our time together at the end of his life turned a corner in our relationship, and I've stayed close to Marie since then. But on my arrival back in the States in 1995, I was grieving the loss of my relationship with my in-laws almost as much as my failed marriage.

I had to fight to get out of bed every morning and only did so to make sure that Sam was going to her job as a summer camp counselor and to school once the academic year started. I knew she would be fine once she made some new friends. She was the same age as I was when I left Ghana to go to boarding school in Rome. That adjustment had been tough, but I had done it, and I was confident she could, too. I often cried myself to sleep, but what woke me up in the middle of the night and kept me awake most nights was not the overwhelming isolation and dislocation. It was fear. Fear of how we were going to survive financially on my meager alimony and child support from George.

Part 2: Metamorphosis

I knew I had to find a job and fast. However, that was not so easy without a professional network and with a multifaceted global résumé that didn't fit easily into American boxes. While I was in Geneva, I had worked with Dr. Robert (Bob) Westphal at the International Federation of Red Cross and Red Crescent Societies, editing a quarterly newsletter called *Transfusion International*. He moved back to Boston shortly before I did and introduced me to a contact of his, and as a result, I was hired as the editor for the *Harvard Center for Blood Research Newsletter*, a part-time gig that lasted two years. In the meantime, Bob asked me to edit the third edition of his American Red Cross handbook, *Transfusion Medicine*. Through a former colleague of George's at WHO, I landed a part-time contract as an editor at Management Sciences for Health. Soon, I had more freelance work than I could handle, which definitely helped to ease my financial insecurities. I could finally sleep through the night again.

I slowly broke out of my social isolation as well. Through the introduction of a mutual friend, I met Effie Maniatakis, a Greek-American elementary school teacher who lived in the same Blue Stone condo complex I did. Effie and I met to take a walk around Braintree, leading to countless walks over the years around Pond Meadow Park and on Nantasket Beach in Hull. She began including me in gatherings of her friends. I also began to meet eligible men through events at my local chapter of Parents Without Partners. Sam disapproved of all the men I dated (she still harbored hopes that her father and I would get back together), except one she called "Mr. Cookie Man" because he always came to pick me up armed with a plate of cookies he had just baked. I joined the Boston chapter of the Appalachian Mountain Club (AMC) and hiked almost every weekend all over the greater metropolitan area, in places like Blue Hills and Middlesex Fells.

With Effie (far right) and her friends on her birthday

On a hike in November 1995, four months after I moved to Braintree, I slipped on some wet leaves, twisted my right ankle, and ended up breaking it. I was in a cast and on crutches for six weeks. Sam wasn't old enough to drive yet, and I had to take taxis everywhere, even to the nearby subway station or to go grocery shopping. The timing couldn't have been worse: I hobbled into an interview I had at the Harvard Family Research Project (HFRP) for a position as part-time editor-in-chief for their newsletter, *The Evaluation Exchange*. It was snowy and icy; getting around was treacherous even for the able-bodied. I think I got the job because the executive director was impressed by my sheer determination to get all the way to Cambridge and up the spiral staircase to her office for the interview! By the time I started working at HFRP in January 1996, my cast had come off, and I wore just a clunky orthopedic boot. I commuted to Cambridge three days a week. It took an hour each way on a packed subway that snaked its way under downtown Boston until it emerged to cross the Charles River. I got to know the layout of Boston through its underground subway stops long before I ever glimpsed the neighborhoods above ground.

By the following spring, I was back to doing some easy hikes. I eventually led a few hikes and volunteered to compile the monthly list of hikes for AMC's newsletter. On one of these hikes, I met Mary Lou Kirkpatrick. We chatted as we hiked, and Mary Lou asked if I played tennis. At that point, I was grateful just to be walking and wasn't at all sure running around a tennis court would be possible. Besides, I hadn't played since I left the Philippines more than 10 years earlier. Mary Lou invited me to just hit some balls on the court at her condo. The rest is history, both our friendship and my ongoing tennis obsession. Mary Lou and I joined a competitive league and also played socially at the Weymouth Club. From then on, much of my social life revolved around the club and included trips with fellow members to play on the grass courts at the Tennis Hall of Fame in Newport, Rhode Island, and to watch matches at the U.S. Open in New York City.

With Mary Lou at my family's summer cottage in Gloucester, 1997

I continued to work part-time at the Harvard Family Research Project until my contract ended, but by then (a year and a half after our arrival), Sam had settled in, and I felt less anxious about leaving her as a latchkey child. In January 1997, I applied for and was selected as a full-time project manager in communications at a nonprofit in downtown Boston called Jobs for the Future (JFF). I wrote, edited, and produced publications in the fields of workforce development and education. During the summers, when work at JFF slowed, I dropped back to part-time and continued to freelance, writing articles for two magazines, *Booming* (geared to seniors) and *Taste for Life* (on health and lifestyle issues). Sometimes the editors assigned topics, and sometimes I proposed my own, but I loved the research, interviewing, and writing that went into each article. I found I could write about anything, even how to decorate a patio or deck ("Organizing Your Oasis") when I had nothing but a couple of Adirondack chairs on mine! It was the first time since I freelanced in Manila, more than 10 years earlier, that I felt fully creative.

I was also rejuvenated by reuniting with my college roommate Christiane Corbat Westlake (she used her maiden name professionally, but the surname of her husband, Bob, in her personal life). We had seen the Westlakes over the years, not only on their visits to Switzerland but also on our biennial home leaves. We had stopped to see them either at their home in Barrington, Rhode Island, or at the Corbat family farm in Vermont. Our two families were extremely close. We attended each other's weddings, traveled together as newlyweds to vacation in Chincoteague, Virginia (where George and I later bought a small parcel of land), and rejoiced at the births of our respective children. Christiane was godmother to our son Chris, who was named in her honor. Time seemed to have erased all the conflicts we had in college — after all, I was no longer hanging out with the wrong crowd or smoking! Christiane's art had taken an abrupt turn. She was now working with natural materials, like feathers, wood, and stone, producing American Indian-style dreamcatchers and tapestries. She was also creating body-cast sculptures to symbolically represent the transformation of illness, personal crisis, and other adversity. The dollhouse sculpture she did of me (a reference to Ibsen's play and my newfound independence) was exhibited at the University of Rhode Island and other venues. She later created a sculpture of intertwining hands to symbolize the marriage of our son Chris and daughter-in-law, Carolyn. (Christiane officiated at their wedding ceremony on June 25, 2005, in Nantucket, a year before she died.)

"Outgrowing the Doll's House" by Christiane Corbat

Christiane's home in Barrington and her studio in Warren were both about an hour-and-a-half drive each way for me, but I went to visit as often as I could, especially to celebrate our birthdays in April (midway between mine on the 19th and hers on the 29th). I also joined the Westlakes one year on their annual summer trip to Cold River Camp in New Hampshire; this was a hiking camp with cabin living and communal dining in the White Mountains. (At Cold River Camp, I met Alan, a man I dated for about a year before he decided to retire — solo — to his family's estate in Kennebunkport, Maine. It was an incredibly sweet relationship while it lasted, and we've continued to stay in touch a few times a year.) I'm not a great sailor, but I occasionally went sailing on the Westlakes' 28-foot sailboat, *Zelda*. There's a Chinese proverb that says, "One may have friends all over the world, but very few will truly know your heart." Spending time with Christiane, who was a healer (a graduate of the Barbara Brennan School of Healing), as well as one who knew my heart, did wonders for my psyche as I tried to put my divorce behind me and move on both personally and professionally.

I spent four years at Jobs for the Future, but workforce development and education weren't really my fields of interest.

With Christiane, Cold River Camp, summer 1996

So, in 2000, I found a new position as a staff writer and project manager at Relocation Resources International (RRI). This global company helped American expatriates move from one location to another, handling everything from accommodations to schools for their children, and from language lessons to setting up bank accounts. We had real estate agents, educational consultants, moving companies, and personal assistants in nearly every major capital in the world. If a Fortune 500 company executive and family had to move from Paris to Tokyo, everything was done for them, down to packing and unpacking their belongings. My experience moving around the world served me well in this position. However, as an adult, I had never had anyone to hold my hand throughout the process. I wrote articles about relocation issues, set up international conferences, liaised with vendors worldwide, and produced brochures and marketing collateral in eight different languages (with the help of translators and field representatives).

Part 3: *Adventures by the Boatload*

During the time I lived in Boston, I had the opportunity to travel both for work and pleasure. RRI hosted an international conference every year, and soon after I started working there, I got to go to one in Dublin. It was my first trip to Ireland, and I was smitten. Dublin was fascinating — a juxtaposition of Irish history and culture, like daily performances of plays by George Bernard Shaw or Samuel Beckett, and hip twentysomethings out enjoying the nightlife. To orient myself before the conference started, I took a hop-on, hop-off, double-decker bus tour of the city and was able to get a bird's-eye view of the sights, including the famous Ha'penny Bridge and the Guinness Storehouse that included daily tours of its factory and tastings. The conference was held during business hours, so I had the evenings free to sample some of Dublin's pub food, like Guinness Stew. I stayed on an extra day to go to Northern Ireland to have lunch with my former parish priest, Father Peter, in Belfast, about three hours each way by train. He was visiting his family in his hometown of Magherafelt, a 40-minute car ride outside the city. My first trip to Ireland was short-lived, less than a week, and I promised I would get back and soon.

Fortunately, Ireland wasn't far from Boston — a mere six hours — and Aer Lingus had daily flights back and forth. I returned to Dublin that summer and then headed west for two separate walking tours, one of Connemara and the other on the islands off the west coast. In Connemara, I stayed in a rustic Irish inn and took daily hikes to places like Kylemore Abbey, with its magnificent Victorian walled garden. My fellow travelers were all local Irish wanting to enjoy the natural beauty of the area. My second walking tour was more international, with travelers from all over the world. I kept in touch with two women, one Japanese and one German, for at least a decade after our tour. Every morning, we would take a ferry to a different island, not the Aran Islands but small, sparsely populated islands with names like Inishbofin (population 180) and Inisturk (population 50). We would hike all day, carrying a packed picnic lunch, and then have supper at the island's only pub, always accompanied by local musicians playing tourists' favorites, like "Oh, Danny Boy" and "When Irish Eyes Are Shining." The islands were rustic and peaceful, although the weather could be unpredictable. It was August, but we often experienced all four seasons in one day.

On my way to the west coast by bus, I went through my father's ancestral village of Arva (population 411) in County Cavan. Then I returned to Dublin via Galway, where I spent the day roaming the city's streets, visiting the Galway City Museum and people-watching in Eyre Square, a public park that dates back to the 18th century. It had been officially renamed John F. Kennedy Memorial Park. In addition to other statues, the park has a portrait bust of JFK, who was much beloved by the citizens of Galway following his visit there in 1963.

By the end of my two trips to Ireland, I felt fully immersed in its geography, culture, folklore, and gastronomical tradition. The Irish people were incredibly hospitable, often stopping and asking me if I was on a heritage trip, then quite popular among Americans searching for their roots. I wasn't officially. I hadn't done any in-depth ancestry searches, but on some level, I had always been curious about my father's heritage and his side of our family since it was less spoken about than my mother's.

I returned to Geneva for brief visits several times in the early years after my relocation. The first time was only months after I had left. In retrospect, it was much too early, long before I had had time to adapt to my new home. However, my parishioner friends at John XXIII had given me a roundtrip ticket on Swiss Air as my farewell present. They were worried I would be lonely during the holidays and wanted me to come back to spend Christmas with them. It was a lovely gesture, if ill-timed for me. I wasn't ready emotionally for the visit, and my broken ankle, while healing, was still encased in its clunky orthopedic boot. Swiss Air put me in a bulkhead row and provided a small, collapsible stool on which I could prop my ankle during the long flights to and from Geneva. (I would have preferred an upgrade to first class, but beggars can't be choosers!) While I was happy to see my son Greg and my friends again, it made it all the harder to return to Boston after my brief visit. My next trip, about 18 months later (in the summer of 1997), was much easier and more satisfying. Greg lent me his car (the small Peugeot I had bequeathed to him on my departure), and I was able to get around — including hiking in Verbier and a visit to Taizé, where I met up with Father Peter who was driving to Ireland for his annual leave. I was on the road in France when I heard about Princess Diana's car accident in Paris (August 31); her death dominated the news nonstop until I left. Just over a year later, in October 1998, I went back to Geneva again. That would be my last trip until 2015, some 17 years later, a clear sign that I had moved on, slowly but surely, from my previous life as a married woman in that Swiss city.

All my travel wasn't international. I attended the wedding of my sister Kathy to John Brown in Silver Spring, Maryland (where she was born), in September 1996. The following year, when Sam was a junior in high school, we began her U.S. college tours. On her spring break, we went to visit the University of Colorado, Boulder (where Greg had been a student for a year), and to California to visit Pomona College, Claremont McKenna College, Marymount College (now Marymount California University), Santa Clara University, and the University of San Francisco. (She had already visited the University of San Diego and Loyola Marymount University with her grandparents the previous summer.) In July, she joined me at the conclusion of a work-related conference in New Orleans; we visited Tulane University and Loyola New Orleans. On weekends throughout the spring and summer, we drove all over New England, visiting, among others, the University of Massachusetts Amherst and Connecticut College, where Sam took one look at the main administration building and refused to get out of the car for our scheduled tour. She said it looked too much like her high school. We had, of course, been to

Dartmouth a few times to visit Chris while he was an undergraduate, including a trip to ski with him and their cousin Jamie (my sister Kathy's son). I took advantage of our tours to write and publish an article, "A Private College: Your Best Choice," in *Private Colleges and Universities*, a glossy magazine sent to the parents of high school students throughout the U.S.

I was able to travel for my freelance work as a writer as well. In early 1999, the Government of Canada invited me to go on an all-expense-paid trip. I flew into Quebec and, after an overnight, was taken by van with other travel writers to the Laurentian Mountains (highest point 3,825 feet) to witness firsthand some of Canada's amazing outdoor winter activities — mushing with dog sleds, snowshoeing, skiing, riding snow mobiles — and amenities — award-winning restaurants and spas. We were brought back via Montreal, where we spent another overnight and were lavishly wined and dined with Canadian specialties, like caribou and poutine, and dishes flavored with maple and juniper berries. In return for the government's hospitality, I wrote several travel articles. Most were rejected because my trip had been paid for, and therefore, I was not an unbiased reviewer. I ended up getting just two articles published, "Running with the Dogs" in *Booming* (print magazine) and "Wining and Dining in Quebec Province" in *Time To* (online magazine). I'm sure the Government of Canada had hoped for more, but I certainly did a lot of word-of-mouth publicity about this French-speaking, and thus more exotically foreign, part of Canada so close to Boston.

While I had longed to travel after moving back to the States, I also wanted to make a difference in the world. The opportunity came when I heard about a nonprofit organization called Global Volunteers, which has different types of programs in countries all over the world. So many of them sounded interesting and fulfilling, but I settled on its program to teach English in Vietnam. I signed up for what is known euphemistically as a "volunteer vacation," a two-week assignment in Cao Lãnh, a provincial town outside of Ho Chi Minh City, for October 2001. A month before we were due to leave, the September 11 terrorist attacks occurred. Some of my fellow volunteers backed out, but we ended up with a group of 12. I flew first to Bangkok to stay with my friends MV and Mike O'Neil, who were there from Geneva on a three-year assignment. I had been to Bangkok a couple of times on business in the 1980s, but that was two decades earlier and much had changed.

While Mike was working, MV and I went out to explore and enjoy Thai massages. Although MV had a car and driver, we got around on the Skytrain, an elevated rapid transit system that ran high above the city, and tuk-tuks, three-wheeled motorized rickshaws that would weave in and out of the megacity's horrendous traffic. MV and I then traveled together to Siem Reap for a few days to visit Angor Wat and other temples in northwestern Cambodia; it felt like we were on the set of an Indiana Jones movie. We did tons of touristy things in and around Siem Reap, like riding an elephant in the jungle. As always, we laughed a lot. (Unfortunately, we didn't make it to the capital city, Phnom Penh, about 200 miles away.) When our brief visit to Siem Reap was over, I took off for Vietnam.

Riding an elephant with MV in Siem Reap, Cambodia, October 2001

I flew into Ho Chi Minh City (formerly Saigon) and was met by a local Global Volunteers representative. She took me to the hotel where I would meet up with my fellow volunteers who came from all over the U.S. After a day of briefings, we set off by bus to Cao Lãnh, more than three hours away, in the Mekong Delta region of the country. We were housed in a small hotel near the middle of town and given our assignments. I had requested to work with adults and was assigned to the community college teachers. Their written language skills were excellent, but their spoken English, with a thick Vietnamese accent, was almost incomprehensible. As the language school was quite far from the hotel (too far for me to walk), one of the young male community college teachers would pick me up on his motorcycle and drive me back after class. We rode without helmets (Vietnam had no helmet law until 2007), and I always sighed with relief when I made it back to the hotel in one piece. As my classes were in the late afternoons and evenings, I helped out during the day at the local middle and high schools. These classes were extremely pedagogical, diagramming sentences and the like, and not nearly as much fun as mine with the community college teachers, which focused on conversational language skills; our exchanges were freewheeling and informative.

With students in Cao Lãnh, Vietnam, October 2001

It was such a privilege to get to know these young Vietnamese, all born after the war and who had no animosity toward Americans.

On the contrary, they admired the U.S., and all wanted to visit, if not immigrate, here one day. They were compassionate toward us, knowing that we had just lost more than 3,000 of our citizens in the 9/11 terrorist attacks. Their words of condolence brought tears to my eyes, as they came from people who were our sworn enemy when I was in college. Visiting their museum, I gained a new appreciation for the country that had endured so much — decades of wars with China, France, and the United States. I found it ironic that the Vietnamese called the war with us "The American War." On one of our days off, we rode in wooden rowboats down the narrow inlets off the Mekong Delta. It was easy to see how the Viet Cong could evade our troops between these hidden jungle waterways and the infamous underground Cu Chi tunnels.

During much of the rest of our touring, we were up to our mid-shins in water. It was the rainy season in Vietnam, and that year the rains had been particularly heavy; there was flooding everywhere we went. Nonetheless, it was an incredible trip, like no other I've ever taken. It combined mission, camaraderie, and adventure in a country that I had previously only known through newspapers and TV coverage in the 1960s and early 1970s. (One of my fellow volunteers, Jerry Gastrand, and I have kept in touch for 20 years. I connected with him and his wife, Elaine, in Florida, and they came to visit me in San Diego.)

On my way back to Boston from Vietnam, I stopped in Kansas City, Missouri, for the memorial service of my aunt Dorothy, my father's sister, held on November 3. (She had died in July of Alzheimer's; I don't know why her service was delayed for four months.) Dorothy Hewson Green Dreher was one of my favorite relatives. She visited us regularly in Chevy Chase when I was a child, and I connected with her on several occasions when I was an adult, including when she visited us in the Philippines. A graduate of Smith College, she worked in publishing in New York City and, for many years, as an elementary school teacher in the Kansas City public school system. She loved books, libraries, and writing. We shared so many interests, all except her passion for birdwatching. My father had died the previous year, so the only remaining members of that side of the family were their two half-sisters and their families, most of whom I had never met before and have not seen since. Aunt Dorothy's passing felt like the end of an era: she was the last of that generation of relatives I knew as a child.

Part 4: California Dreaming

When I returned to my job at RRI after three weeks away, I found out that 9/11 had changed everything. Following the terrorist attacks, many Americans lost interest in living abroad. For a few weeks, the company was busy moving families back to the States, and once that was done, business fell off dramatically. RRI limped along for a while but then started laying off staff. As one of the newest hires (there only 14 months), I was laid off at the end of November 2001. Had I known I was going to be laid off, I would not have rushed back from Asia.

I survived on unemployment insurance and income from my freelance writing. I took advantage of my extra spare time to become certified as a Kundalini Yoga instructor. My friend Effie had dragged me to my first Kundalini Yoga class at our local high school years before. It didn't grab me at first, but once it did, I was hooked for life. I enrolled in a 200-hour training program that took place on weekends over an academic year at an ashram in Millis, about an hour's drive southwest of Braintree. After I graduated, I began substitute teaching in classes around Boston and Providence. However, it wasn't enough to make ends meet, and I knew I had to combine it with more lucrative work.

I grappled with what I was going to do next. My layoff gave me the opportunity to switch gears, and Sam's graduation from college freed me to relocate if I wanted to. I did some serious soul-searching. As much as I loved Boston and the friends I had made there, I couldn't stand the winters. We had had two particularly cold and snowy ones. The snow had piled up so high in the grocery store parking lots in Braintree, they had to truck it and dump it in the Charles River. I longed to live in a place with pleasant weather all year round — Florida or Southern California?

I had helped to plan and manage several national and international conferences with both JFF and RRI. With that experience under my belt, I volunteered to work at several conferences, including one in Miami so I could check out Florida as a possible new place to live. Once the conference was over, I visited South Beach, then friends from Geneva who lived in Key Biscayne, and finally Jerry Gastrand who was living in Venice. I crisscrossed the state in my rental car, checking out employment opportunities and housing options. I knew the Orlando area from several visits there, including one for a conference and one to take Sam to Disney World for her 12th birthday. (I had given Sam her choice of any Disney theme park in the world, including Paris, Tokyo, and Hong Kong, and she had picked Orlando.) My look-see visit convinced me that I would be happier in San Diego, where two of my kids had been living — Greg working at the Ralph Lauren boutique in La Jolla and Sam attending her sophomore year at the University of San Diego.

I started applying for jobs in San Diego and flew out for a flurry of interviews. I got an offer from Rady Children's Hospital Foundation, my first choice, where I ended up working for seven years (2002 to 2009). It was the best job ever. I was the editor of *Rady Children's Magazine* and wrote content for fact sheets, press releases, and the hospital's website. I prepared talking points, speeches, and PowerPoint presentations for donor cultivation and recognition events and for annual meetings. I volunteered to work at dozens of these events, many held in the evening or on weekends. I served as liaison with *The San Diego Union-Tribune* for an annual advertorial section called Kids' News Day. I loved writing patient stories for both the magazine and Kids' News Day. I met the most amazing kids — from toddlers to teens — and their families, and it was such a privilege to be able to tell their stories, many of them nothing short of miraculous. I did in-depth series on various parts of the hospital, like the trauma unit and the cancer ward, and got to know the place inside out. It made me so proud to take a prospective donor on a tour of "my" hospital. I cared deeply about Rady Children's Hospital and my colleagues at the Foundation.

Given that I knew no one when I first moved to San Diego, it's not surprising that many of my early friends were colleagues from Rady Children's, like Lisa Reddy and Debbie Williams, with whom I still walk on a regular basis. (My kids had both left San Diego before I finally got here; Greg had moved to Portland, Oregon, and Sam had returned to Massachusetts and graduated from Stonehill College.) Gradually, I began to meet people outside the office. I met Sue Macdonald while hiking on a Sierra Club singles outing. We continued hiking together over the years, later with the Canyoneers (through the San Diego Natural History Museum) and MeetUp. We were involved in a host of other activities together — we ushered at the San Diego Symphony, played tennis at Balboa Tennis Club, which I joined my first week in San Diego, and for a while (pre-pandemic), challenged each other to do something different every single weekend for a year. We did some fun things, like taking the Palm Springs Aerial Tramway to Mount San Jacinto to snowshoe and the ferry to Catalina Island to go ziplining. We traveled together to Indian Wells once a year to watch tennis, camped out in a tent at a Sierra Club Halloween party in the Foster Lodge in Mount Laguna (now closed due to fire damage), went hiking around Lake Tahoe in 2018, and the following year, walked the San Diego Half Marathon with our friend Tony. Over the nearly two decades of our friendship, it would be impossible to count the number of things we've done together: concerts, ballets, theater performances, movies, and dinners out in restaurants spanning the length and breadth of San Diego County.

With Sue, Mount Woodson, New Year's Day 2018

Through regular playing, leagues, and socials at both the Balboa and Coronado tennis clubs, I met even more friends, including a few male ones whom I dated briefly. However, it was difficult to date at this stage of my life. I had been badly hurt by my divorce from George, and at the same time, few men measured up to him. Over a span of more than three decades, George and I had shared some unique experiences, starting with our global upbringings and continuing through the raising of our three children. Most of the men I dated, first in Boston and then in San Diego, had no understanding of what it meant to live overseas, unless they had served in the Peace Corps or in the military deployed abroad, but even that was not comparable. One San Diegan man, on breaking up with me, said pointblank, "You're too sophisticated for me." (I think he meant worldly wise, but I wasn't going to quibble with him.) This man had never been out of the United States, not even to Canada or Mexico, and had no desire to. His bucket list included all 15 presidential libraries and all 63 national parks in the United States, and he was more than halfway done. While I wouldn't mind visiting these libraries and parks, with or without him, I knew I needed a man with a larger worldview.

I really enjoyed my life in San Diego, and I still do. However, for a brief time, I toyed with the idea of moving to San Francisco. I missed the vibrancy of a real city, and I knew it would be more cosmopolitan and cultured than San Diego. During the two years Chris was doing his MBA at Stanford, I went several times to Palo Alto to visit him and Carolyn and then later to various parts of the Bay Area for job interviews. I was never offered anything more appealing than the job I had at Rady Children's and found the cost of living there even more exorbitant than in Southern California. I eventually gave up my search and accepted a relocation to San Francisco just wasn't in the cards — or in my best interests.

Part 5: More Adventures by the Boatload

When I returned to the States in 1995, my goal had been to take at least one international trip a year. I met that goal in the early years and then some, for example, traveling to both Ireland and Thailand/Cambodia/Vietnam within one year (2001). After I moved to San Diego, however, I wasn't able to travel internationally as much, partly because I used my meager vacation days to visit my young grandchildren and partly because most of my disposable income went into saving for, and ultimately buying, my first condo in 2003. During the seven years I worked at Rady Children's, I only managed to squeeze in two international trips, one to Spain (with brief stops in Paris and Geneva) and one to China.

While we were living in Europe, I got interested in the various pilgrimages there. I started researching them and ended up writing and publishing an article, "Off the Beaten Path: Pilgrimages in Europe," in a local Geneva publication, *The Courier.* George, Sam, and I had taken the overnight train to Lourdes in southwestern France to visit the miraculous Grotto of the Apparitions, and we had gone to Einsiedeln in Switzerland to see the Black Madonna in the Benedictine monastery there. We had also hiked six hours up the mountain to the Hospice of the Grand St. Bernard for an overnight stay and prayer vigil at the monastery. The only way we could get Sam to hike that far was to promise she could pet the famous St. Bernard dogs that are bred there. (The boys had adamantly refused to go on any of these pilgrimages.) One of the pilgrimages I had written about in 1993, but had never done myself, was the Camino to Santiago de Compostela in the Galicia region of northwestern Spain. I finally made it 11 years later.

The Camino, known as the Way of St. James, is a network of pilgrimage trails leading to the shrine of the apostle St. James the Great in the Cathedral of Santiago de Compostela. My friend Marianne and I decided to join a group based in France for a one-week trip in August 2004. In retrospect, this was probably not the wisest time to go: it was a Holy Year (when the feast of St. James, July 25, falls on a Sunday), so some 180,000 pilgrims made the trip that year, and August is always the busiest month of the year on the Camino. However, once we started walking, we were oblivious to the others on the Camino. I had flown into Paris, taken an express train to Geneva, met up with Marianne, who lived not far outside the city, and then flew with her to Spain. We started our Camino in the small town of Sarria, 125 kilometers (about 77 miles) from Santiago. One has to complete at least 100 kilometers (about 62 miles) on foot to earn a *compostela* (pilgrim certificate), and we were doing slightly more than that. We were a small group of walkers, about 12, including our guide, coming mostly from France and Belgium. Marianne and I were the only nonnative French speakers, but both of us are fluent and had no problem fitting in. Most pilgrims are on their own quests, either recreational or spiritual — or, in my case, a combination of the two.

With Marianne along the Camino, August 2004

Every day had a similar routine. We ate a simple breakfast of bread and coffee, picked up a packed lunch, and left our luggage in front of our accommodations, usually a small guesthouse or country inn. (Most pilgrims stay in primitive, dorm-style "refugios," but we had opted for a more upscale tour.) We walked an average of 10 to 12 miles a day through beautiful eucalyptus forests, farmlands, and rustic villages. Along the way, we went into local churches or stopped to buy water at a bar or convenience store. At one such stop, an Australian man asked me, after finding out I was from San Diego, "How does an American like you end up walking with a French group on a pilgrimage in Spain?" I wasn't sure exactly how to answer, but it certainly was serendipitous! We took our time, stopping for snack and lunch breaks, and usually reached our next overnight stop by 5:00 p.m. Most of my fellow walkers took long naps, but as I am not a napper, I watched the Summer Olympics (held August 13–29 in

Athens) on Spanish television. I couldn't understand everything, but I got the gist of what the announcer was saying. Around 9:00 p.m., we would begin our dinner — hearty Spanish meals with plenty of red wine — and often not get to bed until midnight. They were long days but immensely satisfying, physically, culturally, spiritually, and gastronomically.

After walking for six straight days, we arrived in Santiago de Compostela (population 10,000). The cathedral towered over the town. As it is the largest Romanesque church in Spain and one of the largest in Europe, we were awestruck to look up at this immense manmade structure, especially after a week submerged in nature. Inside, we watched in amazement as a giant incense thurible on ropes was swung by eight priests across the main altar. We then visited the crypt beneath the altar to see the Tomb of the Apostle St. James, said to contain his relics. Afterward, we went to the office to receive our certificate (we had had our pilgrim passports stamped at each stop along the way to prove we had made the pilgrimage) and a scallop shell, the iconic symbol of the Camino. On Sunday morning, we attended mass at the cathedral and had a final light lunch at a nearby restaurant. It was sad to say goodbye to our guide and fellow walkers; we had spent a wonderful week together. Marianne and I flew together to Paris, where we had dinner at one of her favorite restaurants (now mine!). The following morning, we parted ways — Marianne back to Geneva and me back to San Diego. It was yet another one of our many shared memories. In the past, we had traveled together to Mexico (where we got food poisoning in Ensenada), to Las Vegas when her son had lived there, and countless places in Switzerland to hike and cross-country ski.

It would be a while before my next international trip. After Christiane died in August 2006, Bob Westlake and I kept in touch, sharing our grief and our memories of her. About six months after her death, Bob signed up for a *locum tenens* position (temporarily replacing a psychiatrist on sabbatical) in Phoenix, Arizona, partly to escape the house he and Christiane had shared for their entire marriage and partly to do something different from his work teaching psychiatry at Brown University. He invited me to visit him one weekend in Phoenix and thus began a rather bizarre, whirlwind relationship in which we tried to transform a friendship of 40 years into a romance. Despite the fact that he had grown up on a farm in Pennsylvania, we had a lot in common. He was liberal-minded and well-read, enjoyed classical music, had traveled some — at least around Europe and once for an extended stay in New Zealand — and had a good, if somewhat sophomoric, sense of humor. We were both looking for companionship and, ultimately, a committed long-term relationship. In some ways, ours looked like a match made in Heaven. We spent glorious weekends together in both Phoenix and San Diego — attending concerts, watching sunsets at the beach, and eating in nice restaurants — and took short trips to places like Sedona to hike and explore new vistas as a couple.

While Christiane was alive, she had spoken often about wanting me to guide her and Bob on a private tour of China. She was one of the only, if not the only, person who had read every single article I had written about China. Every few months, I sent her a packet with my latest articles, partly for her to read and partly to have a complete set of my portfolio safely stored outside the Philippines. Unfortunately, we never had the opportunity to take that trip together. So, once Bob and I had been dating for a while, but he was back in Rhode Island, we decided the two of us should take Christiane's dream trip. By that time, I had been to China at least a dozen times, but Bob had never been anywhere in Asia before. Planning a trip to satisfy both of our needs was challenging, especially since we agreed that we would split the costs of the trip. We started squabbling before we even booked our trans-Pacific flight. He wanted to fly first class, which I couldn't afford. He ended up paying the fee for extra legroom for both of us for the 12-hour flight from San Francisco, where we met to start our journey.

I decided our first stop in China should be Beijing because of its political and historic significance. This was a year before the Summer Olympics were to be held in Beijing (starting at 8:00 p.m. on 08/08/08, eight being an auspicious number in China), and the authorities had already begun a campaign to clean up the air. Nonetheless, when we landed at 2:00 in the afternoon, it looked more like dusk, with the sun just barely visible through the thick smog. We had agreed we were going to see the "real" China, but as soon as we walked outside the airport terminal, Bob was overwhelmed by the horde of people and balked at riding a public bus or the subway. We ended up taking a taxi into the city. I knew from that moment, the trip would be difficult for Bob, and it was.

Once we checked into our hotel and got to our room, Bob went straight back to the registration desk to get an upgrade. This pattern would continue throughout the trip, at every hotel and even on the boat when we took a three-night Yangtze River cruise. I had made all our reservations through China International Travel Service (CITS), a state-owned company based in Beijing, and they seemed fine to me. I wasn't going to complain about staying in nicer rooms, but neither was I going to pay half of the upgrades. Bob's China trip ended up two or three times more expensive than mine! Bob also had trouble with the food in China. It didn't look or taste anything like what he was used to in Chinese restaurants in the States. I coaxed him into eating some traditional meals, like Beijing duck in one of the famous restaurants in Beijing and hot pot in Chongqing, a megalopolis of more than 30 million people at the convergence of the Yangtze and Jialing Rivers in southwestern China. He was not an adventuresome eater: for breakfast, he ate badly cooked scrambled eggs while I savored a bowl of steaming *conjee*, a type of rice porridge, with side dishes of steamed buns and dumplings.

I dragged Bob to every tourist site in Beijing — from Tiananmen Square and the Forbidden City to the Temple of Heaven, and from the National Museum to the Drum Tower. I ended up hiring English-speaking guides at each site because he had more questions than I could answer. We took a rickshaw tour of the *hutongs* (alleyways in the old part of the city), and I finally got him on the subway to go outside the city to visit the Summer Palace, the summertime resort for the Qing dynasty's royal family. I was tired of going to the popular Badaling section of the Great Wall, so I arranged for us to be dropped off at Jiankou, about 50 miles outside Beijing, at sunrise and picked up at Mutianyu at sunset. The distance between Jiankou and Mutianyu is only about six miles as the crow flies, but the wall zigzags on steep mountain ridges and, in some parts, has disintegrated so badly we had to climb off the wall and walk along it, but at least we ran into very few people along the way. The views from the watchtowers in this section were gorgeous. This was definitely one of the highlights of our two-week stay in China.

Hiking with Bob at the Great Wall, September 2007

I made only two mistakes in my meticulous planning for this trip. The first involved our Li River cruise. It clearly states online that there are only one-way cruises from Guilin to Yangshuo and no cruises from Yangshuo to Guilin. However, at the time, I didn't know that. When I asked the CITS representative if we could travel up the Li River, she said it wasn't usually done, but she didn't see why not. It turned out to be an eight-hour trip, twice the time of the down-river cruise, and we had no services, not even a cup of hot tea. The staff were off duty, and most were sleeping soundly. One of them felt sorry for us and scrounged up some leftovers from the down-river buffet luncheon. The latter part of the trip was in darkness, so we missed seeing some of the more dramatic, craggy karsts (hills formed by limestone rock). When we finally arrived at the boat dock, there were no taxis. We were stranded about an hour's drive outside of Guilin. I negotiated in my poor Chinese to have one of the staff's cousins meet us there and drive us to our hotel, a ridiculously expensive ride because of the late hour and distance.

My second mistake took place at the end of our Yangtze River cruise. (What is it about river cruises?) We had started our cruise in Chongqing, traveling downstream through the Three Gorges — a succession of three spectacular canyons — before ending in the city of Yichang. Since I was still trying to get Bob to experience the "real" China, I insisted we take a public bus from Yichang to Wuhan, now well-known as ground zero for COVID-19. I was really proud of myself for having gotten us on the correct bus, and it was indeed an authentic experience, complete with peasants taking produce and chickens to market. I had never been to Wuhan before and had no idea how big and sprawling it was. It's the most populous city in Central China, with a population of over 11 million. I heard the bus driver announce that we had arrived in Wuhan, only to find out, after we had disembarked and the bus had departed, that we were on the outskirts of the city at the first of three city stops. Once again, we were stranded. I was finally able to find a taxi willing to take us to our downtown hotel. To me, these mistakes were all part of the travel adventure; to Bob, they were extremely irritating. I sensed he was used to being in control and was thrown off by the lack of it in China.

Bob was the most content when we based in Guilin and made several day trips from there. One was a day of hiking along the Longji Rice Terraces, about 60 miles outside of the city. Bob was relieved that there were no direct buses to Longji so we could travel in relative luxury in a hired private, airconditioned car with driver. We chose the Jinkeng ("Golden Hollow") area, home to the Red Yao ethnic minority. We hiked to the Huangluo Yao Village, known as the "World's Longest Hair Village." The women with super long black hair, up to five feet in length, dress in traditional ethnic costumes. They were more than happy to have their photos taken for a fee. In retrospect, for Bob's sake, I probably should have planned more outdoor activities away from the maddening crowds and given us more time to luxuriate in the beauty of China's countryside.

On our flight back to San Francisco, we were exhausted and a bit cranky, even with the extra legroom. Over each of our heads were little thought bubbles that read, "Where do we go from here?" I don't remember now who actually articulated the question, but we finally faced it head on. Even though we had convinced ourselves that Christiane would have approved of us dating, her ghost was with us every step of the way — during our six months together before this trip and even more acutely in China, as this was "her" trip. Moreover, Bob was 10 years older than me, ready to retire, an avid sailor (so avid he was annoyed about having to put his boat away for the winter due to our trip's timing), and unwilling to leave New England or, at that point, consider selling his house in Barrington. I had moved to San Diego five years earlier and wasn't thrilled at the idea of returning to the East Coast, especially Rhode Island. I suggested several options, including spending part of the year in New England, preferably Boston, and the rest in San Diego. He was willing to do another *locus tenens* position in San Diego or elsewhere, but only temporarily. As we delved deeper, it was clear Bob was fine with a friends-with-benefits kind of relationship, while I was looking for some sort of commitment if I were to pull up stakes again. We talked for hours but got nowhere. We were stalemated. We hugged and said goodbye at the San Francisco Airport. I flew back to San Diego with silent tears streaming down my face and the words of my friend Effie in my head, "If you want to know if you're compatible with someone, travel together for a week or more." She had been right. Bob and I had discovered that we were not compatible on the issues that mattered most to us. I have not seen him since, although we usually exchange cards at Christmas.

Domestic trips were of course interspersed with my international ones, especially for family gatherings. Unlike the 1994 British rom-com, *Four Weddings and a Funeral*, I attended two weddings and three funerals in the early 2000s: Greg's wedding to Kim Tallman at a riverside cabin outside of Portland in July 2004; and Chris's to Carolyn Wolff at her parents' summer home on the island of Nantucket in June 2005. My father's memorial service was held in Silver Spring, Maryland, in April 2000, followed by a committal service in Gloucester in September of that year; my ex-father-in-law Leon's requiem mass was held in Tucson in November 2004; and Christiane's celebration of life took place in Providence in August 2006. Three deaths in six years may not sound like much, but these were three very important people in my life, and I was overwhelmed by grief. I was especially affected by Christiane's death because she had been so young (only 61 years old, the same age as my mother when she died), so healthy and so vibrant until the year before, whereas my father and my ex-father-in-law were both in their 80s — my father, 89, and Leon, 86 — and both in failing health.

There was some comfort in the words of Ecclesiastes (made popular by The Byrds' 1965 hit song, "Turn! Turn! Turn!"): "To every thing there is a season... A time to be born, and a time to die...." The joy at the births of my grandchildren did indeed mitigate some of the grief of these deaths and gave hope for the next generation: Greg and Kim's children, Hannah (February 2003) and Noah (January 2006), and Chris and Carolyn's children, Eliza (July 2007) and Samuel (November 2009). I traveled frequently to both Portland and Houston to visit my grandchildren until they were old enough to come visit me on their own as unaccompanied minors. I also traveled to Tucson every May to celebrate the birthday of my ex-mother-in-law, Marie.

Visiting Marie on the occasion of her 93rd birthday in May 2016

You would think that all these trips — both domestic and international — would have satisfied my urge to travel. However, I was still restless, both personally and professionally. I really did care deeply about Rady Children's, and I might have stayed there for the rest of my career if it had not been for a powerful seven-year itch that propelled me in a completely different direction.

Part 6: Off to Serve My Country

One weekend, on a group hike in early 2009, I met a woman who was about to take off for an assignment with the American Red Cross in Iraq. I was intrigued; the assignment sounded so exciting and exotic. I asked her to send me more information. Before I knew it, I had obtained a high-level security clearance, quit my job at Rady Children's, rented my condo, and was on my way to Washington, D.C., for training with the American Red Cross's Service to the Armed Forces. I had worked with the Red Cross, both nationally and internationally, but had no idea that, since 1900, the American Red Cross has been tasked with supporting our military overseas. The six weeks of training in D.C. was intense, much of it computer-based. Then we were on to Fort Benning, Georgia, where we learned, among other things, how to avoid stepping on an IED and to administer battlefield first aid. We were given vaccines against every possible disease and biological warfare agent, like anthrax. We flew to our assignments via Kuwait, where we slept in tents in the desert and were issued our equipment, including a tactical vest and helmet that weighed 30 pounds and 6.5 pounds, respectively. Once loaded up with all my gear, a backpack, and two duffel bags full of uniforms and personal effects, I could hardly put one booted foot in front of the other.

I spent five months in Iraq (Camp Liberty) during the drawdown in 2009 and another five months in Afghanistan (Bagram Airfield) during the surge in 2010. In both places, our team of four tracked down and informed a service member's commanding officer of an authenticated family emergency at home, and if it were deemed urgent, such as a dying parent, we would arrange for transport back to the States. We maintained a welcoming lounge with a large library of both books and movie DVDs, with microwave popcorn to enjoy with them. We had an unlimited stock of personal care items sent from well-wishers at home; I lugged the care packages from the post office to our van and back to our office for distribution. At Bagram, I made rounds at the hospital, offering a smile and giving out phone cards and a kit of personal care items, including warm socks (Bagram sat at nearly 5,000 feet and was cold in the winter). I stopped visiting the ICU: I couldn't bear to see so many strapping young American men with arms and/or legs blown off, and I was sure, given their high level of sedation, they wouldn't remember if an American Red Cross representative had been there to give them a toothbrush.

Some aspects of serving in Iraq were actually fun. Camp Liberty was part of a larger complex of interconnected bases, and we were able to move freely from one to the other, thus varying our mess halls and PXs. We had a community that included Iraqi-American translators, many of them from San Diego (one of the largest concentrations of Iraqis in the U.S.), and contractors from various vendors working on base. There were American food outlets (which we avoided), such as Pizza Hut and Taco Bell, and several Iraqi restaurants and hookah bars, plus an outdoor concert stage and a dance hall. I kept really busy. In addition to my eight-hour shift, seven days a week, I walked around the artificial lakes and canals in a lovely area that used to house Saddam Hussein's many palaces and hunting grounds. I taught yoga at one of the gyms and volunteered on weekends with the military's Catholic Church, a vibrant faith community inspired by the enthusiasm of the Chaldean Catholic translators.

On deployment in Afghanistan, 2010

I enjoyed working with my team in Iraq; we were tightknit and respectful of each other. I had a sharp learning curve since I had no military experience at all and couldn't even distinguish the ranks of the people I met (I spent hours memorizing insignia). It was complicated by the fact that we were part of an allied force, with service members from many different countries, all with different uniforms and insignia. Our team rotated shifts, and I only minded the midnight to 8:00 a.m. one. It threw off my sleep and meal schedule and left me feeling discombobulated. That shift was especially challenging in Afghanistan where our team was not cohesive, and I was housed in a flimsy B-hut with only six-foot-high plywood dividers between our beds. Women came and went at all hours or tried to Skype — shouting loudly ("Can you hear me now?") — with their loved ones, especially their young children, back home.

While we had had occasional rocket and mortar attacks in Iraq, we were bombarded frequently in Afghanistan. Once in the predawn, our base was breeched by Taliban insurgents: one wearing a suicide vest blew himself up at the gate, allowing about 30 of his fellow attackers to enter. As the sirens went off, I jumped out of bed, donned my boots, helmet, and vest over my pajamas and headed to the closest bunker. I huddled there for what seemed like hours, listening to the sound of bullets zinging by as helicopter gunships and soldiers in watchtowers fired on the insurgents dressed in stolen American military uniforms. The attack left one American contractor and 10 Taliban guerrillas dead, a dozen soldiers wounded, and me very grateful to be alive.

I promised myself that I would never take anything for granted again — not a hot shower, a comfortable bed, silence at night, privacy, freedom from concertina wire, or even a hot cup of coffee in the morning. And in the weeks and even months after I returned from Iraq and Afghanistan, I didn't. I appreciated every moment and relished all the little pleasures of life. I had no patience for my friends who complained about their commute or some other mundane aspect of their life. I wanted to shake them and say, "Don't you know how lucky you are?" As time went on, however, the memories of hardship and deprivation began to fade. I, like everyone around me, would start to grouse if I had to wait too long in a supermarket line. Nonetheless, the experience of the two deployments was important, not just in developing an attitude of gratitude. It fulfilled my pent-up desire to do something adventuresome and my enduring passion to make a difference in the world — even if that world was no bigger than a military base in a foreign land.

Part 7: Blooming Where Planted

I toyed with a third deployment. The American Red Cross suggested Djibouti next, since "things were heating up in Africa." As tempting as it was, I figured it was time to stay home for a while and spend more time with my grandchildren. At that time (mid-2010), they were age 7, 4, 3, and nearly 1 year old, two in Portland and two in Houston. I had met the youngest, Samuel, when he was a newborn on my way back to San Diego from Iraq the previous year. I also missed spending time with my friends. We had kept up superficially via email while I was on deployment, but it's not the same as hanging out and communicating face to face. I would stay "home" and take advantage of all the things I had missed while I was living in war zones.

I landed a job working remotely as a social media content writer for TPR Media, based in Boston. I wrote 144-character tweets for Twitter and longer postings for Facebook, all promoting a healthier lifestyle. It was creative and challenging, especially trying to distill well-researched wisdom down to a limited number of characters or words.

Around this same time, my friend Duke Doudna and I opened a yoga studio in Hillcrest. I had started teaching Kundalini Yoga at the Y in the evenings after work within a month of arriving in San Diego in 2002. I taught in a small mind-body annex in Mission Valley that has since been closed. I started teaching one class a week and then two, a schedule I kept up continuously until my deployments, and again on my return. Duke took classes from me at the Y and eventually became an instructor himself. We both dreamed of having our own dedicated studio and decided to make it a reality. We spent months looking for a suitable place to rent, writing our business plan, choosing a name (Yoga Oasis), hiring instructors, and marketing our classes.

Teaching Kundalini Yoga at the Y, May 2011

We opened Yoga Oasis with much fanfare in summer 2010 and, for a while, were going great guns. We taught all types of yoga, not just Kundalini Yoga, and some specialty classes, like yoga for kids. We had some topnotch instructors from all over the world. Unfortunately, things began to go downhill in and around the building where we leased our studio, including the opening of what turned out to be a very popular lesbian bar and restaurant below us, which created an intolerable level of noise and whose patrons filled all the adjacent parking spots. Homeless men began sleeping at the entrance to the staircase leading up to our studio and were already camped out before our evening classes let out. The final straw was when our landlord reneged on a promised remodel. We were able to break our three-year lease early (with a substantial payout), and we closed our studio less than a year after we opened it. Duke and I were devastated, but we learned a lot about being small business owners and managers and what it means to follow one's dreams.

I had decided it was time to go back to work full-time, and while Duke managed our yoga studio singlehandedly, I started a new job as senior writer at UC San Diego Health Marketing and Communications. It was a good fit. I enjoyed the camaraderie of my colleagues, and I had a great supervisor, Jennifer Arevalo, who has remained a friend to this day. I was using many of the researching, writing, and editing skills I had honed at Rady Children's. However, the collateral was focused on marketing with promotional information about UC San Diego Health's services, not its patients. I missed the more human aspect of fundraising collateral, and after two years in Marketing and Communications, I jumped at the chance to transfer to Health Sciences Development (still at UC San Diego) with a promotion to director of communications, with my own staff of writers and designers and a substantial increase in both responsibilities and salary.

A few months before my promotion, in September 2012, I took my second "volunteer vacation," this time to Shanghai with Projects Abroad. I had considered moving to China to work for a year or two, and I thought a one-month program would give me a good idea of what it would be like to live in China as a foreigner. Up until then, my visits had usually lasted only two or three weeks each. Given my writing and editing skills, I was assigned to a gorgeous, glossy bilingual magazine called *iMetro*, which showcased once a month, current happenings in the worlds of art, culture, fashion, and food in Shanghai. I wrote seven feature articles that were published in the October issue, covering topics from a local film festival to a staycation in Shanghai. I was usually bylined with one of my Shanghainese colleagues, although they merely translated my article into Chinese and didn't add anything to the content.

I was responsible for mentoring the much younger and inexperienced staff whose translations into English read like they were taken directly from Google translate and were almost incomprehensible. They were resentful of my presence and my attempts to help them. They deliberately ostracized me during their tea and lunch breaks and refused to even talk to me, except to give me assignments. I had hoped to improve my spoken Chinese during my month-long stay, but hardly anyone spoke to me, even in restaurants and shops. If they did, it was always in English. I learned a number of important lessons: the Chinese youth I observed had zero social skills, even among each other; they were more comfortable texting than talking. Living and working nine-to-five in China was not much different than anywhere else, except for the food and the round hole in the gleaming white floor tiles in the restroom in lieu of a toilet. And most importantly, I knew at the end of the month I didn't really want to relocate to China after all. I returned to San Diego happy to be back and looking forward to my new position in Health Sciences Development.

Working in the iMetro *office, September 2012*

My two years as director of communications were undoubtedly the highpoint of my professional career. My bosses — especially my direct supervisor, Nathan Chappell — were supportive and inspiring. The sky was the limit, and my staff and I responded in kind, producing award-winning print collateral for events, campaign materials, and videos, as well as proposals and stewardship reports to assist frontline fundraisers. In 2013, I co-authored a proposal that resulted in a $100 million gift to create the Sanford Stem Cell Clinical Center, the second largest gift in UC San Diego's history. Given my innate shyness, I could never have been a fundraiser myself and approached a donor directly. But I was persuasive in my writing and adept in providing the frontline fundraisers what they needed to do the ask. I would never not be shy, but I had found a way to transform my introversion into professional success. The following year, my staff and I were instrumental in helping Health Sciences Development achieve what had been considered an almost impossible goal of raising $131 million for a building, the Jacobs Medical Center, including the successful completion of a $25 million challenge match.

No matter how busy I was at UCSD, I continued to teach yoga twice a week in the evenings at two different branches of the Y. I had been teaching for more than a decade when I decided I wanted to take the next level of Kundalini Yoga teacher training, which consisted of five 60-plus-hour modules. Since I had been teaching meditation in my classes for years, I chose to take the "Mind and Meditation" module first. I could have taken this module almost anywhere, in San Diego or in many nearby locations. Never being one to take the easy way, I signed up for an intensive week-long course in India, taking place in early 2014 at an ashram in Rishikesh in the Himalayan foothills beside the Ganges River. (Rishikesh was made famous by the Beatles' stay in 1968.) I chose this course partly because of the location and partly because of the instructor, Gurmukh, whose classes I had occasionally attended at her studio in Hollywood on a Sunday day trip or at the annual Sat Nam Fest.

It took me nearly 30 hours to get from San Diego to New Delhi via Frankfurt on two back-to-back 12-hour flights with stopovers. I stayed for a few days by myself in New Delhi in a charming guesthouse, Shanti Home, a veritable oasis in the middle of this bustling megacity. I went sightseeing around the city, including the walled city of Old Delhi and its newer sections. I was particularly moved by a visit to Birla House, where Mahatma Gandhi was assassinated in 1948. On one of the days, I rented a car, driver, and guide to take me on a day trip to Agra to visit the Taj Mahal. It was nothing short of magical to see this iconic ivory-white marble mausoleum in person. It was definitely a highlight of this trip.

Visiting the Taj Mahal, February 2014

I then rode a train to the station nearest to Rishikesh, and in the absence of any public transportation or even any taxis, I accepted a ride from a touter in an unmarked vehicle to go to the ashram. We drove through the Rajaji National Park, which can only be crossed in daylight due to marauding herds of wild elephants. I had expected the worst traveling in India by myself, at the very least "Delhi belly" since I ate at food stalls and even on the train. But I was pleasantly surprised. While I had some challenging moments, like trying to step through thousands of sleeping bodies in the predawn hours to get to my track (one of 18) in the New Delhi train station, there were none of the usual traveling mishaps.

My "Mind and Meditation" course was, well, mind-blowing. There were 40 of us in the class, including 20 Russians who spoke no English and brought their own interpreter, and the rest who came from all over the world. My roommate was a twentysomething

Egyptian woman. We were in our classroom at least nine hours each day, starting with morning sadhana (a daily spiritual practice) at 4:00 a.m. Fortunately, the teaching was highly interactive, and the lectures were interspersed with both small and large discussion groups. We also practiced meditation, some of which seemed endless. There were times when it was hard to concentrate: chattering monkeys would jump in through the open windows, grab any fruit or whatever they could find, and dash back outside. It gave new meaning to the expression "monkey mind" (when your mind becomes easily distracted by random thoughts). At sunset, we would walk down to the edge of the Ganges River, where monks would chant and we, along with Hindu pilgrims and other international visitors, would light candles in little reed boats with flowers and float them on the water as darkness fell.

Sixteen months later I was on the road again, this time with my granddaughter Hannah on her first trip to Europe. Hannah had studied at the French School in Portland, and from the time she was in kindergarten, I promised I would take her to France when she was 12. Not long after that birthday, in June 2015, we flew together from Portland to Paris, where we met up with my Houston daughter-in-law, Carolyn, and my other granddaughter, Eliza, about to turn eight. We stayed in an apartment in Le Marais, once the city's Jewish quarter and now the home of hip boutiques and galleries. The four of us did every touristy thing there was to do in the city — from snapping pictures in front of the Eiffel Tower to taking a Bateau Mouche ride along the Seine. Carolyn arranged a private visit to the Louvre, which the girls loved, and afterward we visited the nearby Tuileries Garden and Orangerie Museum. We were fortunate to have toured Notre-Dame Cathedral before it closed following the April 2019 fire. We took a trip outside the city to see Versailles, which was completely overrun with Japanese tour groups. In the evenings, we ate at trendy restaurants selected by Carolyn, who is a food and wine connoisseur.

Hannah and Eliza at Versailles, June 2015

It was fun to see Paris through the eyes of a 12-year-old, and I made her speak French whenever possible, for example, when ordering an ice cream cone in the park. At times it was exasperating, such as when Hannah was more interested in the Africans hawking selfie sticks on the steps of Sacré-Cœur than in the famous basilica itself, or when a text from a friend at home had her mind in Portland instead of Paris. But all in all, she was an excellent travel companion. Our time in Paris flew by, and before we knew it, we were on the TGV (the express train) to Geneva.

After we parted company with Carolyn and Eliza at the Geneva railroad station, I dropped Hannah off for a brief visit with her grandfather, George, and his second wife, Buena. Yes, that Buena — the same Filipina who had enchanted him in Manila nearly three decades earlier. They had married in 2010 after Buena's husband had died and George's long-term, post-divorce relationship had ended; they now lived most of the year in Geneva. All three of our kids had attended their wedding but found this new relationship a bit awkward, especially Sam for whom Buena had morphed from her godmother to her stepmother overnight. And it was certainly awkward for me to be around them. I took off as quickly as I could, but not before giving them some suggestions for what they could do with Hannah, such as visiting the Olympic Museum in Lausanne.

With MV, riding electric bikes, around the outskirts of Geneva

I stayed with my friends, the O'Neils, in Bellevue and as always, we picked up right where we left off. MV and I walked and rode electric bikes through the vineyards on the hillside behind their house. I luxuriated in views of Lake Geneva and Mont Blanc from the park across the street from their house, at sunrise with a cup of hot coffee and at sunset with a glass of chilled Saint-Véran. Once I retrieved Hannah, we went to stay with my friend Marianne in Vevey, near

Lausanne. She took us, among other places, to the Cailler/Nestlé chocolate factory in Broc, the lakeside statue of Charlie Chaplin (he was once a Vevey resident), and a cheese factory in Gruyères, where we used to take our out-of-town guests.

Hannah and I then headed to Reykjavík, the capital and largest city of Iceland. We stayed in the adorable Butterfly Guesthouse, walking distance from the center of town. As it was June, close to the summer solstice, we had no real nighttime darkness. It became dusky for a few hours after midnight, but that was it. Thank goodness for blackout shades! Reykjavík is well organized for tourists; the main information office had dozens of buses heading out to its premier sightseeing destinations. On the first day, we went to see an impressive waterfall, a geyser (we learned that the word is derived from the Icelandic word *geysir*, meaning "to gush") and a national park. On the second day, we did a city tour, taking in sights, such as Hallgrimskirkja, the largest church in Iceland, with 360° views, and the National Gallery of Iceland. And on our last day, we took a 40-minute bus ride to the Blue Lagoon, a geothermal spa famous for its steamy mineral-rich, blue-colored water and soft white silica mud; there, we spent time relaxing before our return flight to Portland. I came back to San Diego tired but totally satisfied with our two-week, three-country, multigenerational trip of a lifetime. After all the traveling, it was almost a relief to go back to the daily grind at work.

Part 8: Brief Abode in the City of Angels

My work and my team's successes at Health Sciences Development did not go unnoticed in San Diego and beyond. In the summer of 2015, shortly after my trip with Hannah, I got word through a headhunter (a first for me!) that the Vice Chancellor at UCLA's Health Sciences Development wanted to interview me for a newly created position: senior executive director of communications. I was not particularly interested in moving to Los Angeles. However, the position would involve managing an even larger staff, a total of 12 writers, editors, designers, and event planners, and a six-figure salary (another first for me!). I wouldn't have given it serious consideration, except the tightknit Health Sciences Development team at UC San Diego had begun to unravel with a slew of departures, a common occurrence in the fundraising world once a massive goal has been achieved. I reluctantly accepted UCLA's offer and, once again, packed up my condo and rented it out with a one-year lease. I found an adorable duplex in Westwood's Little Persia neighborhood with an Iranian Jewish couple as my landlords and next-door neighbors. It was walking distance to and from my office on Wilshire Boulevard, my new gym, tennis club, church, public library, and dozens of restaurants, mostly Persian but interspersed with Asian and European ones.

I took full advantage of my year living in LA. I went to Disney Concert Hall for the LA Philharmonic and the Hollywood Bowl in the summer with my former colleague and friend Debra Kain who, like me, had relocated from San Diego to LA. I hiked with various groups in the surrounding hills and canyons. I joined a French-speaking foodie group, eating at a different restaurant every month. And I visited almost every museum and place of interest, even the tarpits when my grandchildren visited. I had lots of visitors, including family and my friend Sue Macdonald, who often drove up from San Diego, and my friends MV and Mike, who flew in from Geneva to visit their daughter who also lived in LA.

I was also able to squeeze in one more international trip in 2015, this time to Costa Rica with Sam between Christmas and New Year's. Sam wanted to relax after her busy fall semester at Chapman University, to sit on the beach or on our hotel patio and drink tropical cocktails, while I wanted to get out and explore the country and its many wonders. We ended up compromising as we traveled from Liberia to the west coast and then to the interior: some beach time interspersed with a half day snorkeling off the back of a beautiful sailboat, a half day of hiking through a lush rain forest, crossing numerous very scary suspension bridges, an overnight stay near the Arenal Volcano, and ending with a relaxing afternoon at a natural springs park. Despite our differences, Sam and I enjoyed our stay, especially our evenings, watching the sunset and eating delicious dinners of fresh, local ingredients. Neither one of us was in a hurry to fly back to LA.

With Sam, Costa Rica, December 2015

I relished working with my team of 12 at UCLA, even though we were often stressed out and worked overtime in the evenings and on weekends to meet unreasonable deadlines. UCLA's Health Sciences Development was never able to raise the kind of funds we did in San Diego, in spite of their department being twice the size and the donors in LA being 10 times wealthier. It drove my boss insane. She was a taskmaster and a bully, very unpleasant to work with, to the point I was getting ready to report her for harassment and a toxic workplace. Things came to a head in June 2016 when, in a late Friday afternoon meeting with HR, we agreed that I would retire from the UC system, after less than one year at UCLA, with a pension and benefits, as long as I refrained from suing either my boss or UCLA. It was a very sad and ignominious ending to my five-year career in the UC system.

I stayed in LA for the rest of the summer since I had already paid my rent there and my condo in San Diego was leased until early September. I took a quick trip to Boston to visit friends Effie and Mary Lou and then spent the long Fourth of July weekend in Nantucket with Chris and his family. Once back in LA, my granddaughter Hannah came for a visit, and we had a wonderful time together. We hiked up near to the Hollywood sign and visited the Griffith Observatory. We took a double-decker bus tour of Hollywood, stopping for ice cream at a place known for celebrity sightings (we didn't see any). Sam, Hannah, and I went to the Wizarding World of Harry Potter at Universal Studios and, later that evening, to the movies. After our trip to Paris the year before, Hannah was used to jam-packed days and nights with her grandmother!

In early August, I took off on a long-planned trip to Canada with Mary Lou. We met up in Vancouver, where we went sightseeing and had dinner at the beautiful home of my cousins Anne and Alan Savage.

With cousins Anne and Alan Savage at their home in Vancouver, August 2016

Mary Lou and I took the ferry to Victoria Island to visit the sights there, including the fabled Butchart Gardens. Then we boarded the Rocky Mountaineer, a special tourist train with upper-level dome windows and outdoor viewing areas. The train traveled only during daylight hours, stopping at dusk every day so we could spend the night in a hotel and not miss any of the scenery along the way. We overnighted in Kamloops and Jasper and ended our train ride in Banff. In each of these three rustic towns, we had great fun — exploring places of interest, hiking around, and eating dinners in local restaurants. From Banff, we took a bus to Calgary, nicknamed "Cowtown." Unfortunately, we missed the Calgary Stampede, which takes place in July every year. We took a night tour of the city, including going to the top of the Calgary Tower, a 626-foot freestanding observation tower in the downtown area. The next morning, I flew back to LA, and Mary Lou traveled on to Toronto before returning to Boston.

With this 10-day Canadian trip at the beginning of the month, I had time on my hands for once. I visited some places in LA I had missed during my year there, like the Getty Villa (I had been a couple of times to the Getty Museum but not the Villa). One of the most surprising places I had somehow missed was the cemetery, Westwood Village Memorial Park, which was walking distance from my house but hidden away between high-rise buildings. It is the final resting place of some of the most famous stars in Hollywood, including Marilyn Monroe, Kirk Douglas, Dean Martin, Natalie Wood, and Jack Lemmon, just to name a few. Even with my last-minute gallivanting, I had more than enough time to leisurely pack up my belongings and prepare to move on.

Part 9: Back to San Diego, Jiggety-Jig

I had been invited to stay in the LA area and work with some of my former UC San Diego colleagues at City of Hope, one of the top cancer hospitals in the U.S. However, Duarte, where City of Hope is located, was on the opposite side of LA from Westwood. As the commute would have been nightmarish, I would have had to move again anyway to work there. Rather than starting over again in LA, I decided to move back to San Diego but ended up working remotely for City of Hope, writing proposals and reports for donors. It was the best of both worlds: I was able to move back into my condo and work from home, driving up to City of Hope only once for a tour of the facilities and again for some meetings. I continued to freelance for City of Hope for a year and a half (from the end of 2016 to the middle of 2018).

In January 2017, since my freelance workload varied, I started a part-time job at the Cushman Foundation as its administrator. The work at the foundation — giving away funds instead of trying to raise them — was the flip side of what I had done for the last 15 years. I found it interesting to read all the grant applications, learn about these organizations, prioritize the requests, and present them to the Cushman board (three generations of family members, no outsiders) at their monthly meetings. I thoroughly enjoyed taking the Cushman adult grandchildren on site tours to learn more about the work of these organizations and the people who ran them. However, a little over a year after I started, the Cushmans decided they wanted to expand their giving (larger grants to fewer organizations) and needed a full-time administrator. At that time, I was unwilling to give up my other personal and professional pursuits, and in March 2018, we very amicably parted ways.

I took advantage of my extra free time to plan my bucket list trip to Tibet in August of that year. It wasn't easy! Entering Tibet requires a special visa, and foreigners are not allowed to travel anywhere outside the capital of Lhasa without a sanctioned guide. I was not interested in traveling with a large group, especially not an organized tour from the States, so I had my work cut out for me. I ended up flying to Beijing, where I stayed in a guesthouse in a *hutong* for three days. I had been to Beijing dozens of times, so I limited my sightseeing to some of the newer attractions, such as the Bird's Nest and the Water Cube, which were built in time for the 2008 Olympics, a year after my trip there with Bob. I hired a tutor for four hours each day, two in the classroom and two outside, to work on my Mandarin. It was not a very successful venture: my tutor kept addressing me in English, especially when we were out and about, and I had to keep reminding her to speak to me in Chinese.

I then flew from Beijing to Xining, a city of two million on a plateau in Western China, to board a train to ascend the mountain up to Lhasa (altitude 12,000 feet). I had been told that taking the train would help acclimatize me to the higher altitude, but it didn't. I suffered altitude sickness for the entire eight days I was in Tibet, worse when I went out through the mountain passes at 17,000 feet. My guide provided a local remedy: boiling-hot Coca-Cola with ginger. I ate almost nothing, which was probably just as well. The yak dishes didn't smell very appetizing, and there was very little else to eat. I was feeling so poorly I canceled my trip to the Mount Everest Base Camp. I couldn't see driving seven hours each way and sleeping in a tent just to be able to say I had been there. I chose closer destinations, such as Gyantse and Shigatse, visiting a glacier and dozens of the more than 6,000 Buddhist monasteries scattered throughout the country. I ventured on just one longer trip to Lake Namtso, where I spent the night in what was called a guesthouse but was little more than an unheated shack (at nearly 15,500 feet, it was cold even in August), with facilities consisting of a communal trench for a toilet and no running water.

In front of the Potala Palace in Lhasa, August 2018

I flew back to Beijing, and from the moment the plane landed, I felt 100% better. I learned the hard way that I should avoid high-altitude locations in the future and have taken Machu Picchu off my bucket list. I also learned a lot about the Chinese treatment of the Tibetans since Tibet's annexation, euphemistically called the "Peaceful Liberation of Tibet," in 1950. The Tibetans I met were circumspect in what they said to me, as a foreigner, but it was clear that they chafed under Chinese rule — from the five-starred red flag of China flying everywhere in their country down to their car's GPS navigation operating exclusively in Mandarin.

I managed one last trip, this time domestically, before the pandemic restrictions went into effect in 2020. In October 2019, my two sisters and I took a trip together to visit some of the national parks in Arizona and Utah. Eleanor, Kathy, and I met up at the airport in Phoenix, rented a car, and drove to our first stop in Sedona. I had been to Sedona before with Bob in 2007, but this was a completely different experience. The three of us had never traveled together as adults — indeed, the last time we had traveled together was when we went to the Belgian Congo in 1956, more than 60 years earlier. Thankfully, we got along famously and managed to accommodate each other's likes and dislikes. With the time difference (they both live on the East Coast and were three hours ahead of me), we occasionally had to do some juggling about mealtimes and the like, but generally the trip went off without a hitch.

The three sisters at Bryce Canyon National Park, October 2019

We visited Zion and Bryce Canyon National Parks as we drove north from Sedona to Salt Lake City. It was wonderful to be out in nature and to hike in these beautiful parks. We were delighted by Salt Lake City with its iconic Mormon Tabernacle. We attended a performance of the Tabernacle's pipe organ, had lunch at the

150-year-old mansion of Brigham Young, and walked around the edge of the Great Salt Lake, among other outings. We ate dinner at local pubs (where, surprisingly, alcohol was served) and, on our last evening, splurged at The Roof Restaurant on the 10th floor of the Joseph Smith Memorial Building, with breathtaking views of the city. We parted company in Salt Lake City to make our way back to our respective homes. It was a great trip, made all the more special because it was the last for more than a year and a half.

For two years after leaving the Cushman Foundation in March 2018, I kept busy with teaching yoga and subbing at various branches of the Y, as well as multiple freelance writing and editing projects. Then the global coronavirus pandemic struck. In mid-March 2020, a mandatory statewide stay-at-home order was issued, and I was furloughed from the Y — a job I had held for nearly 18 years (with brief breaks when I was in Iraq, Afghanistan, and LA). Like just about everyone else, my life was put on hold. I coped by establishing a regular exercise routine — walking in different neighborhoods with friends (the parks, beaches, and reservoirs were closed), working out with YouTube videos, and doing my yoga. I started teaching yoga on Zoom and have 52 classes — a year's worth of weekly classes — posted on YouTube.

I really missed playing tennis during our lockdown; I only got to play occasionally at a friend's private courts until the clubs opened back up. My friend Debra Kain (who had moved back to San Diego after a longer stay than mine in LA) and I got together regularly to play games, like Scrabble and Qwirkle, outdoors. Later, after we were vaccinated and the pandemic began to wane, we moved our games indoors at her place or mine and added to the repertoire, games like Bananagrams and Rummikub. Slowly, by the summer of 2021, life was beginning to get back to normal. I was rehired at the Y and could finally return to attending outdoor concerts in the park and at the newly constructed Shell with the San Diego Symphony or touring performers.

I am now at a crossroads, trying to decide whether to look for another part-time position or to volunteer with one of the many local nonprofit organizations, or perhaps a combination of the two. I am looking forward to embarking on the next chapter of my life, firmly based in my adopted home of San Diego. I hope this next chapter will continue to be full of visits with family, gatherings with good friends, physical activities (hikes, beach walks), cultural events, creative projects, domestic and international travel, and above all, more boatloads of adventures.

Epilogue

In the 1950s, a Canadian anthropologist by the name of Kalervo Oberg traveled the world. He was a keen observer not only of local cultures but also of how expatriates adapted to living abroad. He coined the term "culture shock," defining it as "the anxiety that results from losing all our familiar signs and symbols of social intercourse." In 1954, he first presented his model of cultural adjustment that included four distinct phases: (1) Honeymoon, (2) Negotiation, (3) Adjustment, and (4) Adaptation.*

For the first 25 years of my expatriate experience, I was oblivious to the concept of "culture shock." I knew there were times I was blissfully happy living in a foreign country and other times when I would be overwhelmed by homesickness, even though I would be hard-pressed to say where "home" was. It was only when I was living in Manila in the 1980s that I learned about culture shock. This was thanks to Gail Rivera. In 1980, she cofounded a nonprofit organization for expatriates called In-Touch, where I took many workshops on a variety of subjects, from time management to life coaching. I learned not only about adjustment to the Philippines but also about reverse culture shock when one returns to one's home country. (I later went on to teach seminars on "Returning Home" in Geneva.)

---

* Note: These phases are somewhat analogous to the five stages of grief described by Elisabeth Kübler-Ross in 1969: (1) Denial, (2) Anger, (3) Bargaining, (4) Depression, and (5) Acceptance. Oberg's came 15 years earlier.

Looking back, I realized that I had had a very short honeymoon phase in the Philippines. When I first arrived, I experienced the typical fascination of a newcomer. I marveled at the beauty of the country, especially Taal Lake, a freshwater volcanic crater lake, and Matabungkay Beach (later to become our home away from home). I enjoyed the slower pace of life and the hospitality of the people. I was curious to try the food, learn the language, and make new friends. The initial euphoria faded with the declaration of martial law four weeks after my arrival. It put me on edge and made me acutely aware of the fact that I was an American living under a foreign dictatorship.

Most literature on culture shock describes the phases in linear terms. It assumes that you would move from one phase to the next until you adapted to your new country of residence, usually within a year or so from arrival. This was not at all how I experienced it. Every time I thought I had adapted fully to living in Manila, something would trigger a negative reaction to the Philippines, and I would cycle through the negotiation and adjustment phases all over again. The negotiation phase is sometimes described as frustration or irritability, but in my case, it was hostility, especially when the trigger involved one of my children.

For example, when I discovered I was pregnant for the second time, I was concerned about how our firstborn, Greg, would react to a younger brother or sister. (Given their cultural preference for sons, predelivery gender identification was not available in the Philippines for fear it might lead to illegal abortions.) One idea I had was to get Greg a puppy to be his special buddy prior to his sibling's birth. A friend bred cocker spaniels, and one of her dogs had just given birth to a brand-new litter. The puppies were adorable, and we let Greg take his pick; he chose a sweet little female, whom he named Buffy. We were able to adopt her when she was six weeks old. It worked! Greg and Buffy were inseparable, except for the few hours when Greg went to preschool. They ate together, slept together, went for walks together. It was heartwarming to watch them — the little blond boy with his little blond dog. Greg was so smitten by Buffy that he was only minimally jealous of his newborn baby brother.

When Buffy was about a year and a half old, our friend asked if we would like to breed her. Our friend agreed to take care of everything, including finding good homes for the puppies we didn't want to keep. On Buffy's last checkup, the vet told me she was due any day and would probably have five or six puppies. That same afternoon, she went missing. At first, I thought she had gone off to find a quiet place to give birth. But as afternoon turned into evening, it was clear she wasn't anywhere in our house or in the compound where we lived. We combed the neighborhood, inquired with people standing around, put up posters offering a substantial reward, and prayed. By morning, it was clear that Buffy had been stolen.

The policeman who came to investigate the theft couldn't believe it involved a dog. Filipinos, unlike some other Asians, don't eat dogs, but most Filipinos don't have a high regard for them either. Many dogs in Manila were kept outdoors as guard dogs and were not considered pets. Rabies was rampant, especially among strays. "A dog, ma'am?" he asked, practically rolling his eyes. "Yes, a dog, but a thoroughbred one with papers who was expecting five or six puppies," I explained. "Each puppy would be worth at least 600 pesos" (about $100 at the exchange rate at that time). I could tell he was trying to do the math in his head. As soon as he figured out how valuable this dog was, his demeanor changed. "Do you have a photo of your dog I could take with me while I investigate?" he asked. As soon as Greg held out the photo, the policeman grabbed it and rushed out the door. Six-year-old Greg turned to me and stated simply, "The policeman isn't going to bring Buffy back. He's going to sell her and the puppies and keep the money for himself."

Wham! I was thrust back into the negotiation phase of my cultural adjustment. Inwardly, I railed against the endemic corruption in the Philippines — corruption that existed at every level, from Malacañang Palace (the president's residence) down to the man in the street, and was particularly insidious among the police force. We carried around a 20-peso bill in our driver's license holder. Whenever we were pulled over (and it was frequently for foreigners and for no apparent reason), the policeman would ask for our license, slide the money out of its holder and into his pocket, give us a verbal warning, and send us on our way. I hated the system. I hated the injustice of it. And with the theft of Greg's beloved pet, I hated everything about the country and its people.

Once again, I would have to claw my way out of the negotiation phase, learning how to adapt and accept all over again. I don't know how many times I cycled through these phases, probably dozens of times. Fortunately, there were years when I loved living in the Philippines. I was satisfied with both my personal and my professional life, and I didn't let the corruption, the poverty, the overcrowding, the filth, the traffic — all the problems of a developing country's metropolis — get to me. I treasured those times when I could appreciate the Filipino people and their culture just the way they were.

I experienced culture shock in Geneva, especially in the early days. Indeed, there are hardly any two countries more different than the Philippines and Switzerland — from the weather to cultural norms, like punctuality. But as described earlier, my life in Geneva cycled between the mundane and moments of pure bliss. My reaction to the Swiss was not as visceral, perhaps because there was less to react to. The Swiss remained aloof, and everything worked so efficiently: I didn't experience the frustration — and irritability — that I often did in the Philippines.

Reverse culture shock was the most traumatic for me. My roots in Chevy Chase had long since been ripped out and couldn't be so easily replanted. I felt that people couldn't understand me or where I was coming from. My good friends have accepted me as a cultural misfit. Whenever they refer to a television show or a piece of music, it's always prefaced by, "You were probably out of the country and never saw/heard this, but..." I've learned more about American pop culture history in the retelling than I did in the experiencing. It's very disconcerting to have these big gaps in my knowledge, both cultural and academic. For instance, I studied Belgian history in the Congo and Maryland history in Chevy Chase but rarely anything useful, like world history and civilizations.

Not so long ago, I attended a friend's milestone birthday party, where we played a guessing game about the celebrant. One of the questions was to identify the three places she had lived. That led to a discussion of the places all the rest of us had lived. The majority of the guests had lived in only one state (California), and when I mentioned that I had lived all over the world and why, one of them asked what a diplomat was. I was stunned into silence. My silence lasted so long that someone else answered the question, giving a thumbnail sketch of the role of the State Department and the U.S. Embassies and Consulates overseas.

How could I possibly explain in a few words at a social gathering the impact of growing up as the daughter of a diplomat? Or what it was like to live as the wife of an international civil servant? (At least now, with the global pandemic, people have heard of the World Health Organization!) These experiences have shaped my life and made me who I am today. This exchange was a stark reminder of how far I have traveled on my journey — from a shy and naïve girl, attending a typical American suburban public elementary school and knowing little about the rest of the world, to a seasoned, well-traveled, and well-informed global expatriate woman who feels at home almost anywhere but has nowhere to truly call home.

Printed in the United States
by Baker & Taylor Publisher Services